# A VIEW FROM THE INSIDE

*On the Front Line of
Afro-American Liberation*

# A VIEW FROM THE INSIDE

## On the Front Line of Afro-American Liberation

An Autobiographical History

Reggie Brown

SALUKI PUBLISHING

Saluki Publishing
1915 University Press Drive
Carbondale, IL 62901

ISBN 978-0-8093-7001-6 (paperback)
ISBN 978-0-8093-7002-3 (e-book)

*Cover illustration*: Vive and Make Smoothe

Printed on recycled paper. ♻

*In the spirit of unending love and gratitude, I dedicate this book to my parents, Mom and Dad, Florence and Charles Brown who from day one provided me with love, support, and understanding. They were there for me whenever I needed them and whom I miss each moment of each day and whose spirit I cherish forever.*

*I also dedicate the book to my comrades: Jimmy, Leonard, Rab, Blood, Don, Gato, Joe, Doc, Fish and House; yes, the ultimate cadre, there's none better.*

*My kids, Make Smoothe, Vive and Big D who fill my life with joy each day, their extraordinary mother Lana. And for the wellness and love in my life today, I thank my caring wife Monique.*

*To all people who have committed their lives to justice.*

*Especially those who toiled twenty hours a day under conditions of immense sacrifice, and many times made the ultimate sacrifice of their lives, to achieve justice for Afro-Americans during the 1960's and 1970's.*

*We will never forget*

## Special Thanks

Special thanks go out to Jyotsna Kapur, Chair, Department of Cinema and Photography at Southern Illinois University, for her assistance and support in getting *A View from the Inside* published.

   Also special thanks go out to Barb Martin, Director of Southern Illinois University Press, whose knowledge and direction has been greatly needed and appreciated.

## Foreword

I first met Reggie Brown while he was at one of his lowest points, but later learned that this remarkable man had written the book you see before you now. I learned that this man who came asking me for work, not a handout, had played an important role in history, in one of the defining struggles of our time. That among other things he is an author, a poet and a rap musician. And that he has through the strength of God and his own will, turned around his own life, as he had fought for the dignity and well-being of others.

Reggie's book is about his story, but it's also about the greatest challenge our county faces: issues of race. I met Reggie as a Connecticut Yankee living in Charleston, South Carolina, where the Civil war began, and my time in the South had made me realize how far we still have to go.

My friend Reggie is a Black man. A former activist in the Black Panther Party, and I'm a white, Republican voter, and even after reading this book I'm sure I cannot truly appreciate the difference in our experiences. Although Reggie and I have never really talked much about my politics, it will be no surprise to the reader that while we see some, probably even many things the same way, my views do differ from his in more than one respect.

But that is the key to our friendship: respect. I hope this book reaches a wide audience of all races, for among its lessons it is hoped it will help to teach us all respect for ourselves and one another.

Robert J.B. Lenhardt, Charleston,
South Carolina, June 17, 2000

## Prologue

It was a miracle I was still alive.

As I lay in my hospital bed, through a morphine-induced stupor, I began to remember what had happened to me, my body shattered and burned by the fiery explosion of a bomb. As an organizer in the Black Panther Party in 1960's America, I was always vigilant against dangers from racists and the police, but I had let my guard down to one of our own. I had been set up.

As I lay there, I thought back to my youth, as a young boy being taught by the nuns in a Catholic school in New York City. I could never have imagined this, or for that matter many of the amazing things that have happened in my life. As a teenager I would witness the rise of a great Black leader like Malcolm X, who rose up, empowered the people, and then was taken from us. That I would become a member of the Black Panther Party, helping to achieve, among many great accomplishments, the establishment of one the first free school breakfast programs in the country. That our cadre was to become the target of paramilitary attacks by an oppressive government, and how we were able in front of a jury of our peers to prove the justness of our cause. No. I could not have imagined that I would have been involved in so great a movement for peace and justice, or that my role and jealousy would make me the target of a would-be assassin's bomb.

I could never have dreamed of the pain I would experience following the explosion, or how I, a high-school track star, would lose his leg in the fight for freedom. Those drugs, first administered to ease my pain, would become a source of suffering and destruction. That despite my injuries I would attend and earn a degree from Columbia University. That my self-medication would subsequently lead me into the seductive world of the drug trade, or how much strength it would take to leave that world behind me.

I write this book not for my own ego (because if actually reveals many of my personal faults), but instead to thank and honor those who gave so much in the struggle for justice. As one who has been there but also has much to learn, I also want to warn our youth about the choices that may seem easy at the time, but which cause great harm to themselves and the ones they love, while helping to perpetuate the status quo. Finally, through the telling of this story, and in the poems and lyrics I include at the conclusion of this book, I issue a challenge and a wake-up call to the complacent Black community, to take responsibility, revive the spirit and fulfill the legacy created by our great leaders in the time of my youth. We owe it to them and to ourselves.

## My Early Years

Many things have been said about New York and for those of us who were born and raised there; it has provided experiences we will never forget. I now understand why many say that if you can make it in New York, you can make it anywhere. It is well known for the street life, fast pace and making money. I can remember at age five the old double-decker buses that used to go up Broadway through Harlem to Washington Heights. That is a pleasant memory of an early period in my life which is in contrast with the awesome changes which I was to face later on.

I was born on July 9, 1948 at Columbia Presbyterian Hospital on the upper west side of Manhattan. At the time the hospital was conducting a study where it followed a group of children born in the hospital and where able early on, to distinguish the gifted children in the group. At age four I was accepted at Hunter Grammar School for the Gifted, to attend the second grade. My mother Florence Brown has always known the need for spiritual growth and decided instead to wait two years and enroll me in St. Catherine of Genoa, a parochial school.

I have fond memories of being an altar boy at Mass, weddings and other special functions. The whole school, that is, grades one through eight, were taught by nuns. They belonged to the Sisters of Mercy religious order. The population of the school was approximately 65% Black, 25% Hispanic and 10% White. The sisters, who were all white, did a very good job with our education, stressing English grammar and compositions and math.

The type of garment worn by the nuns showed only the face, hands and ankles. The dedicated way the nuns worked and their genuine spirituality always made me wonder how they looked in regular clothing.

Discipline and respect were the core attributes of a parochial school education in the early sixties, and still are. Talking out of turn or raising your voice was out of the question. You had to whisper, or even better, pass a note. Even though our subjects were the same as public school, except for religion, English and Math were always given top priority. As a matter for fact, English Grammar and Comprehension was the most intense course I had in school and it carried over from one grade to the next. Nouns, pronouns, adjectives, adverbs, prepositions, dangling participles and more. We wrote, we practiced and we were tested over and over.

Penmanship was next in importance. From 1st grade through the next several grades penmanship was graded and you received a mark on your report card. It was intense and I didn't like it, but I do remember that my penmanship grades were always at the top, even though many of the boys in my classes also had excellent penmanship. The demands and expectations of the teachers were high but most of us achieved and excelled.

When you are young, acceptance is very important. For a while I was uncomfortable having to wear a uniform to school every day. Blue pants, brown oxford shoes, white shirt and blue tie were required. Obviously most of the kids went to public school in sneakers, jeans, whatever. I didn't like standing out, being shy and sensitive, but my block (156th St. between Amsterdam and Broadway) was one of the best blocks in the neighborhood.

As kids all of my friends were really good kids and there was hardly ever a fight amongst us. Cecil, Tyrone, Butch, Bruce, Douglas, Lonnie, Bootsie, Sherman, Nobbie, and boy we really had fun in those days. We played "Booties up," a handball game, in which the first person out had to crouch against the wall and everyone got to throw the pink Spaulding ball at his butt. We also did "top spinning," or spin the top to which the first person whose top stopped had to put his top in the chalk circle in the street. You got to spin your top, throwing it down at the tops I the circle hoping to chip someone else's top.

We also played stickball and my favorite, "Run, Catch and Kiss." In this game we would count to 50 and all the girls in the block would run and hide and whomever you found you got to kiss. Boy, that was great, there was plenty of puppy love and crushes to go around, and we all had our favorite girls we hoped to catch.

In 6th, 7th, and 8th grade I began to excel in track. I ran on the track team, and just being on a team was special because it was an obvious sign of accomplishment. When I graduated from St. Catherine's I attended Cardinal Hayes High School in the Bronx.

## Malcolm X

During my high school years I developed a strong race consciousness. Outside of my father, Charles Brown, Malcolm X became the person to have the most influence on me. Malcolm was a leader in the true sense of the word. He was able to awaken in many Black people a sense of identity. Blacks, then and now, did not have and were in great need of self-esteem and were suffering badly from self-hatred. Unfortunately, self-hatred has permeated the Black community for more than a century.

What Malcolm did was instill a sense of pride and hope, especially for Black males. Slavery and genocide left deep wounds on the Black man's state of mind. However, Malcolm was able to single-handedly transform my way of thinking without me ever getting the opportunity to speak a word with him.

I recall as a teenager going to 125th Street in Harlem to buy clothes and see Malcolm talking to a crowd of several hundred people. Educating and helping masses of people discover their identity and consciousness, as only a prophet could do. I can also remember that fateful day, February 21, 1965. I was sitting at home watching television when the program was interrupted with a bulletin, "Malcolm X the Black Muslim leader has been assassinated at the Audubon Ballroom."

I was momentarily frozen in disbelief and then raced out the door and down the steps. As noted, I lived on 156th Street between Amsterdam and Broadway, and the Audubon Ballroom was located at 166th Street and Broadway. I ran non-stop up to the Audubon but Malcolm had already been removed and taken across the street to Columbia Presbyterian Hospital where he was pronounced dead on arrival.

The people of Harlem were totally stunned because Malcolm did much of the preaching to the masses of Harlem. Malcolm's wake and funeral was held on 147th Street and Amsterdam Avenue.

When I arrived at the wake there was a line that stretched around the block with people waiting to see Malcolm for the last time. I took my place in line and when I walked up to the casket his ruddy complexion was more apparent than ever.

That was the closest I ever got to Malcolm. Even in death you could feel the power of his presence. There were a lot of television media people outside the funeral parlor. As I stood there, Bob Teague, a reporter for NBC was covering the story for the British Broadcasting Company. He stepped forward and asked me what did Malcolm mean to me? Internally I was choking with emotion but managed to say, "They know what they did but they will pay for it."

Even though Malcolm had died we continued to hear him speak. Recordings of many of Malcolm's speeches became very popular. My friends and I would sit around for hours and listen to and discuss what Malcolm's was saying. We paid special attention to the speech "Ballot or the Bullet" and his message about the house Negro and the field Negro. Also the autobiography of Malcolm virtually became "required reading" for all Black people, and still is.

During the summer following Malcolm's death there were riots in many cities, most notably Harlem and the Watts section of Los Angeles. The riots received national coverage due to the extensive damage done and the open conflict between Blacks and the police. Black youth were in open defiance of police, and arming themselves to prove their point.

As a Black youth during this period I remember having mixed feelings about those events, which were considered by many to be insurrections but caused enormous property destruction in the black community under the slogan "Burn Baby Burn." Riots provided an outlet for many years of pent-up rage in the Black community; however they created no positive results.

## *The Black Panther Party*

The year 1966 proved to be noteworthy regarding the Black American quest for self-determination. Huey Newton, Bobby Seale and others came together in Oakland, California to start the Black Panther Party. Land, bread, housing, education, clothing, justice and peace became the Black Panther Party's demand upon America regarding the needs of the Black community nation-wide. The Party was formed in October 1966 and here is its Platform and Program.

## *What We Want What We Believe*

We want freedom. We want power to determine the destiny of our Black community. We believe we will not be free until we are able to determine our destiny.

We want full employment for our people.

We believe that the federal government is responsible and obligated to give every man employment or a guaranteed income. We believe that if the white businessmen will not give full employment, then the means of production should be taken from the businessmen and placed in the community so that the people of the community can organize and employ all its people and give a high standard of living.

We want an end to the robbery by the capitalists of our Black community.

We believe that this racist government has robbed us and now we are demanding restitution for slave labor and mass murder of Black people. We will accept the payment in currency which will be distributed to our many communities. The Germans murdered six (6) million Jews. The American racist has taken part in the slaughter of over fifty (50) million Black people; therefore we feel that this is a modest demand that we make.

We want decent housing fit for shelter of human beings.

We believe that if the white landlords will not give decent housing to our Black community, then the housing and land should be made into cooperatives so that our community with government aid can build and make decent housing for its people.

We want education for our people that exposes the true nature of the decadent American society. We believe in an educational system that will give to our people a knowledge of self. If a man does not have knowledge of himself, then he has little chance to relate to anything else.

We want all Black men to be exempt from military service.

We believe that Black people should not be forced to fight in the military to defend a racist government that does not protect us. We will not fight and kill other people of color in the world who, like Black people are being victimized by the white racist government of America. We will protect ourselves from the force and violence of the racists police and racist military by whatever means necessary.

We want an immediate end to police brutality and murder of Black people.

We believe we can end police brutality in our Black community by organizing Black self-defense groups that are dedicated to defending our Black community from racist police oppression and brutality. The Second Amendment of the Constitution of the United States gives a right to bear arms. We therefore believe that all Black people should arm themselves for self-defense.

We want freedom for all Black men held in Federal, state, county, and city jails.

We believe that all Black men should be released from the many jails and prisons because they have not received a fair and impartial trial.

We want all Black people when brought to trial to be tried in a court by a jury of their peer group or people from their Black communities as defined by the Constitution of the United States.

We believe that the courts should follow the U.S. Constitution so that Black people will receive a fair trial.

The 14th Amendment of the Constitution gives a man a right to be tried by his peer group. A peer is a person from a similar economic, social religious, geographical, historical and racial background. To do this the Court will be forced to select a jury from the Black community from which the Black defendant came. We have been and are being tried by all-white juries that have no understanding of the "average reasoning man" of the Black community.

We want land, bread, housing, education, clothing, justice and peace.

One can see that the Black Panther Party had a specific, comprehensive platform and program. Of the points of the Party program, it is number seven that received all the media attention and was more than any other responsible for shaping the course of events for the Party from 1966 to 1972. By saying, "we can end police brutality . . . by organizing Black self-defense groups . . . ," the Black Panther Party set off an alarm that created a sense of fear on the national, state and local level among law enforcement. J. Edgar Hoover, then-Director of the FBI, labeled the Black Panther Party "Public Enemy #1," to be destroyed at all cost. He consequently created the "COUNTELPRO" Counter Intelligence Program, designated to eliminate Black leaders in general and the Black Panther Party in particular through infiltration, misinformation, incarceration and assassination.

To make its point about the right of Black people to bear arms, Party leadership and members showed up at the California state capitol in Sacramento, where legislators were considering gun control laws. When members of the Party descended on the legislature with pump shotguns and other arms as a show of protest, the Party was thrust into the national spotlight.

I remember watching the evening news and seeing Panthers dressed in black with black berets and guns in hand, saying to myself, "This is awesome" with memories etched permanently into my mind of pictorial accounts of Blacks lynched, hanging from and tied by metal chains to trees with people in a carnival atmosphere; watching televised accounts of Blacks being beaten by police during peaceful demonstrations, bitten by police dogs, sprayed with water cannons and shot dead. I therefore had an overwhelming sense of pride that a group of young Black men and women had emerged to challenge the perpetrators of genocide and oppression against the Black community.

In Oakland, California, Party members would get in cars and follow the Oakland Police on patrol to monitor their actions. It was important to show the black community that they did not have to live in fear and be intimidated by anyone, not even armed police. Many Black youth across America had become frustrated with and tired of the concept of "turn the other cheek," and it was clear that the Panther Party had become, without question, the vanguard of the Black movement.

The power structure and news media wasted no time in lining up so-called mainstream Black leaders to denounce and separate themselves from the ideas of the Black Panther Party. These so-called leaders, or as the Party called them "jackanapes," embarked on a campaign of denunciation, and this tactic was used over and over again.

For example, when you go into any elementary school anywhere in America and see children eating breakfast before starting classes, just remember that it is the Black Panther Party and only the Party that made it possible. How so? Well, the Party realized early on that when a child receives proper nutrition, he or she has a better chance of achieving and retaining learning. Therefore, the Party started the Free Breakfast for Children Program.

Through a wide range of donations a free hot breakfast was made available for any child who wanted it, a significant difference from the cold cereal the Agriculture Department currently provides.

Thousands of Black children around the country participated in the programs due to poverty in their families, and their inability to provide a wholesome hot breakfast every morning.

The news media and some of the so-called black leaders accused the Party of using the Free Breakfast Programs as a forum to indoctrinate the children, to turn them into communists and revolutionaries. While the Party established these programs all over the country, all they did was provide smiling hungry faces with a good meal. The Free Breakfast for Children Program represents an exemplary expression of "love for the people."

The Black Panther Party grew rapidly and established offices in Los Angeles and other cities in California and then across the nation. Most noteworthy were the New York and Chicago offices. With the Party's rapid growth came the inability of the Party to accurately screen the intentions of prospective members. As a result, a massive campaign of infiltration was undertaken through the joint cooperation between Federal, state and local authorities.

New York City had a very active and visible chapter of the Party and consequently its leadership was targeted for elimination. The leadership, known in the media as the New York 21, were indicted and jailed for conspiring to blow up five midtown department stores, several police stations and various public places. Their indictment and wrongful imprisonment could never have occurred without the infiltration of the New York chapter by undercover "agent provocateurs."

One such agent was Gene Roberts, a member of the New York City Police Department's B.O.S.S. (Bureau of Special Services). He infiltrated the Black Panther Part y in July of 1968, with the sole purpose of fabricating a conspiracy to bust the New York Panther leadership. On April 4, 1964, Gene Roberts was sworn in as a special agent for B.O.S.S. Although he was trained as a special agent, he never went to a police academy or walked a beat. Gene Roberts played the part of being a Black activist well enough that prior to his Panther infiltration, he became one of the Malcolm's bodyguards after having infiltrated Malcolm's organization, the O.A.A.U. (Organization of Afro-American Unity).

At that time Malcolm was considered a very serious threat because he had begun to educate Black masses more and more about the right of self-defense and armed struggle. Malcolm also decided to take the oppression of Black Americans before the United Nations, which obviously got the CIA and FBI real busy. On February 21, 1965 when Malcolm was assassinated at the Audubon Ballroom, Gene Roberts was Malcolm's bodyguard and even went so far as to give Malcolm fake mouth to mouth resuscitation.

In 1968 when Gene Roberts infiltrated the New York chapter of the Panther Party it was with the intent of fabricating incidents that would land the leadership in jail with long prison terms. A transmitting device was placed under Gene Robert's skin for the purpose of gathering information that could be distorted for the benefit of a planned prosecution. In order to avoid suspicion, Gene Roberts worked hard and made great efforts to be liked by the members of the New York chapter. He had the Party principles down pat and knew the ideology of the Party like the back of his hand. By March of 1969, with the aid of the New York Police Department, Gene Roberts, along with other agent provocateurs, constructed and fabricated enough lies and madness to give the go-sign for the bust. On April 2, 1969, the homes of more than thirty members of the New York chapter were invaded and the occupants charged with a long conspiracy indictment. Ultimately the case went to trial and all members were acquitted of all charges.

## *Taking a Position*

During the year 1968 I took special interest in following any information and news involving the Black Panther Party. This was also the year I decided to go away to college. In high school, geography always interested me, especially different cities and cultures. I knew even then that I wanted to leave New York to attend college, but I was undecided as to where to go.

The idea of going to California intrigued me, and I had a contact at the University of California–Berkeley, a top administrator who could guarantee my admission but no immediate financial aid. I therefore ruled out California.

A friend of mine, named Riff, was close to graduating from Southern Illinois University. We lived and grew up on the same block on 156th Street. He came home for summer recess and one day we sat down and talked. He showed me beautiful pictures of the university and told me it had a significant black student population with some of the most beautiful Black female students anywhere. I said, "Hey, I'm really interested." I went home, talked to my parents who were very supportive of the idea. I soon found myself on the phone talking to someone in the admissions office. The admissions officer told me that the University operated on a quarter, not semester basis, and that summer quarter would be a good time for me to start. Consequently, I had about two weeks to get ready. I was surprised that I wouldn't have to wait for anything, just come down and they would handle the whole admissions process when I got there. My parents gave me the money I would need to register and cover my tuition for summer and fall quarter. So there I was, my plans laid out, my clothes packed and getting ready to attend Southern Illinois University, in a town called Carbondale.

Carbondale? I didn't even stop to check where it was on the map, but in a flash I was at Penn Station, where the Amtrak trains arrive and depart from. The furthest I had been from home was Washington D.C. to visit my cousins, so this was a big move for me. The train ride was 23 hours long and I had to change trains in Indiana.

When I finally arrived in Carbondale I didn't expect what greeted me. I got off the train, the sun was blazing and I only saw two or three people. The train tracks ran right through the center of town. I left the train station, looked down the street at the clock above the bank, and the temperature registered 106 degrees. Right then I began to have doubts as to whether I had made the right choice.

Who wants to walk around in 106 degree heat? At any rate I had Riff's phone number and he told me who to get in touch with for a place to stay.

Carbondale was a real culture shock for me. I was an inner city youth, who grew up in Harlem, now finding myself in a rural town surrounded by farms and coal mines. Carbondale is located 320 miles south of Chicago near the southern tip of the state. Both Memphis, Tennessee and the Mississippi border are less than 225 miles south of Carbondale. It became obvious that Carbondale, for all practical purposes, was southern. The town of Carbondale registered a population of 20,000 and the student body population at SIU was 22,000. These two populations together made for quite a few people.

I knew right away that I wanted to live in the Black community and not on campus. Out of the 20,000 local residents, approximately 3,500 were Black and lived primarily on the Northeast side of Carbondale. I immediately fell in love with the spirit of the people. If you were Black and lived in Carbondale you always spoke to one another, whether you knew the person or not; if you walked past someone you would always speak. For me, coming from New York, this was a unique and beautiful experience.

When children and youth spoke to adults, it was "yes ma'am," and "no ma'am." I also found it very easy to communicate and talk to people. If a girl liked you she would let you know in a real pleasant "down home" accent. The way girls would pronounce my name really turned me on. I was from New York and that made many girls want to know me; it was great!

There were also approximately 1,800 Black students enrolled at Southern Illinois University. Most of these students came from Chicago, St. Louis, and many other smaller cities in Illinois. There were also several Blacks from around the country, from cities like Denver, Washington D.C., Memphis, Jackson, Mississippi, and other southern cities. Of the 1,800 Black students, the females outnumbered the males 4 to 1, so it wasn't hard for guys to make friends with girls. On campus all Black students also spoke to each other and one could feel a sense of bonding together.

Having been touched by Malcolm X, my consciousness regarding Black people was high, and it brought me in contact with people who were also concerned about Black identity. When I arrived in Carbondale, less than 50 Black students lived on the Northeast side, and unfortunately many black students thought they were better than the local residents, calling them "local yokels."

For me the Northeast side became home and I was able to blend in and develop very positive relations with many people. When I went on campus I was impressed with the enormity of the University which covered several square miles with new state of the art buildings. The student center was a tremendous facility with an escalator, bowling alley, 15 pool tables, 3 cafeterias, a bookstore, several lounges, a movie theater and at least 4 ballrooms that could be used for speaking engagements and dances. It also housed all student government offices and student affairs organizations.

One thing that I noticed was that there was construction going on in several locations on campus and when you read the sign at the construction area it stated that the work was sponsored by the Federal Government. I found this very interesting. Remember, during this period the Vietnam conflict had become tremendously explosive. Southern Illinois University and the federal government stuck a deal that allowed South Vietnam officers to be trained at the University by federal officials. When this became known by the student body, anti-war activists became increasingly busy.

I settled into college life and my classes very quickly, having chosen political science as my major. I was doing well in school and enjoying it. Actually this was one of the happiest and most gratifying times of my life. Living in the Black community I was able to develop good relations with some of the key people on the Northeast side.

One such person was the principal of the Crispus Attacks elementary school. Remembering that the Black Panther Party had been successful developing and running free breakfast for children programs, I got together with some of the young Blacks in the community and we approached the principal about letting us use the school cafeteria on Saturdays to hold a free breakfast program. He okayed it and we were able through donations to create and maintain a breakfast program on Saturdays. So there I was, getting good grades in school and doing something positive in the community. Actually I was having the time of my life.

June, 1969 came quickly and that meant coming home to New York for the summer. It felt great to be home with my family and be back on the block to renew ties with my friends. New York City is much more interesting and tolerable when you've been away from it for a while. Yes, it is truly the city that never sleeps. I don't believe I heard a car horn blow more than a few times the whole year I was in Carbondale. Now, horns were blowing in anticipation of the light turning green letting the driver ahead know it's time to get moving. I enjoyed the sound of kids playing in the street and hearing from my third floor window, girls jumping double-dutch. I always was and still am amazed at the skill displayed by young girls and teenagers taking rope jumping to an art form.

On my block I became a role model. Many of the kids knew I had gone away to college and that gave them encouragement. There was energy burning in my soul, to act, take a position, to do something as a young Black that would be real special. I made the decision that summer to join the Black Panther Party. I somehow had no fear of any of the consequences that could possibly occur. I decided to act, in the spirit of Malcolm, to commit myself to freedom, for Black people "by any means necessary"

## All Jokes Aside

On a Monday afternoon in the middle of June 1969, I jumped on a bus and headed down to 122nd Street and 7th Avenue, the location of the Harlem office of the Black Panther Party. When I arrived on the block I could see the office had a big steel door painted black and was half open. I walked in, introduced myself and said I was interested in helping the Party do community work. I was invited to stay for a political education class that was getting ready to start.

As I took a seat in one of the folding chairs, I felt uneasiness in the air. I realized that with the leadership still in jail due to the Panther 21 conspiracy set-up, it was definitely affecting the functioning of the Harlem office. The Harlem office was mainly functioning to stay afloat while the leadership was in jail.

I remember Charlene, a very articulate and independent black woman leading political education class. It was interesting to see an assertive and politically aware Black woman stand her ground, challenge others and give constructive criticism.

Only on the rarest of occasions did I see anyone in that office smile. Yeah, there wasn't anything funny. My attitude quickly became that of a soldier. I knew I could deal with whatever I was called on to do. My work involved distributing clothes to people in the community, selling the Black Panther Newspaper, and participating in the political education classes.

By the end of July, I was making plans to head back to Illinois as a member of the Black Panther Party. I went to the Party's Field Marshall, D.C., and informed him of my plans and desire to work with the Illinois chapter, headquartered in Chicago. He gave me a letter to give to Fred Hampton, Deputy Chairman of the Illinois chapter. I already knew through news accounts that the Chicago office was very active and the heat was really on in Chicago. I looked forward to meeting Fred, who had already gained national notoriety. In my opinion, outside of Malcolm X, Fred Hampton's leadership ability, commitment to Black people, Charisma, powerful presence and love of the masses was second to none. In one word, Fred was awesome.

The Black Panther Party's main office in Chicago was at 2350 West Madison. The west side of Chicago reminded me of the Brownsville section of Brooklyn, a ghetto, full of Black people and, in terms of class, definitely the lumpen proletariat (below the working class).

I made my way up the steps to the office, announced myself and handed over the letter to the desk sergeant. As soon as Fred appeared, I had a feeling that he was "THE MAIN MAN" in the Black Panther Party. Fred had that beautiful balance of power plus love.

There was a lot of business for Fred to take care of, so we didn't get to talk until late in the evening. When we did, it was all serious and full of meaning. Most of the Panther activity in Illinois occurred in the Chicago area. There were no Panther members in the southern end of the state. I told Fred that I was already very active in Carbondale and had established good relations in the black community. I was also one of the founders of the Black Student Union at Southern Illinois University.

Although Fred had never been to Carbondale, his political vision was so clear that he suggested and I agreed that the best way to organize Carbondale was to utilize the philosophy and programs of the Party without declaring that I was a member of the Party. For Fred and myself what was most important were the needs of the people.

My mission was to start a cadre (a small hand-picked cell), and organize the community. The most important decision for any leader is the selection of the key people. If you have any loose ends you'll be finished before you get started. It has nothing to do with friends or intimate relationships, and has everything to do with character, commitment and accountability. When one is in a position of influence that person's character must be solid as a rock. There is no room for even the slightest improprieties which will be magnified a thousand-fold and destroy the faith and trust of the people.

Your commitment is determined by your sense of purpose. Why are you doing this? Some people joined the Black Panther Party to make themselves appear strong and hide from their weaknesses and therefore not really grow. Some were "arm-chair revolutionaries," intellectualizing and talking but never putting themselves on the line.

During this period there emerged a way of thinking in the Black community that we in the Party called "cultural nationalism." This philosophy was adopted by people whose sense of commitment was to grow large afros, wear the most glowing African dashikis and dresses, talk about Black power, but does nothing that actually helped meet the needs of the people. These people just got in the way, and still do.

Many of today's so-called Black leaders talk about the needs of Black people but compromise in a minute for personal gain. Accountability is essential for the survival of any people's organizations, which means one must submerge the ego and think collectively. It takes very special people to be willing to think collectively. Collective decision-making is too progressive for most people, who only think and act in terms of "I" instead of "We."

## The Crew

Well, the spiritual seed of leadership was planted inside me. I was able to pick only the most trustworthy and "get down" people into the cadre. There was Leonard, a ladies man who had a sophisticated presence about him, always in control, but very down to earth. I approached him about becoming a part of the crew and he expressed a strong interest. Leonard's roommate was Rab. They were not only roommates but real tight. Both were from Chicago and Southern Illinois University students, completely different but the best of friends.

Leonard was from the far south-side of Chicago, a middle class neighborhood of Black homeowners. Rab grew up in the projects. The two of them alone made a formidable team. Rab had a great sense of humor but was not to be messed with. I let him know what I was putting together and he simply said, "O.K. I'm down."

For about a month the three of us worked closely together. I knew we would need at least two more rock solid people, so I kept my spiritual eye open. When one has a discerning spirit it enables the individual to get the feel for a person from a distance. To discern means to recognize visually or mentally with keen understanding. To distinguish a person's intentions and be attentive is vital for success in organizing a strong unit of people.

The ability to discern brought me to Jimmy. He was a sophomore student at the time, and we would always acknowledge each other upon sight. He was always carrying a lot of books but I knew he was more than a studious intellectual. We began to talk and he left no doubt that as articulate as he was, he was at his best when in action.

As a young teenager he belonged to the Black P. Stone Nation, a powerful and notorious Chicago street gang. The Stones recruited youths as young as 9 years old and their oldest members went well into their forties. Jimmy's sister Elaine had the presence of mind to have Jimmy move in with her since she lived in a quieter neighborhood on the south-side. As a result he was able to finish high school and be admitted to Southern Illinois University. Jimmy was a person that would not be intimidated by anyone, and having developed black consciousness he became a true warrior and Black revolutionary.

By 1969 Black power was a political philosophy embraced by many Black groups nationwide. At universities across the country, Black students organized Black Student Unions and were recognized as legitimate student organizations which allowed for use of university facilities and access to university resources. As one of the founders of the Black Student Union at SIU, it put me in a position to obtain needed resources to develop and strengthen Black Panther activities in southern Illinois.

Southern Illinois University was unique in many ways. At the same time the university was training South Vietnamese army officers, it was being utilized by Black activists to empower the local Black community. It also had an active and powerful chapter of SDS (Students for a Democratic Society), made up of young white radicals who were at the forefront of anti-war movement, as well as being strong supporters of the Black Panther Party.

The university was also unique in that white students elected a Black student as student body president. Dwight Campbell was one of the most articulate young Blacks on the American scene. He also had the ability to forge a coalition of majority white student support. By this time, Southern Illinois University was approximately 25,000 students with 1,800 Blacks. Dwight was elected by a landslide and became a leader in terms of the anti-war and Black power movements.

In Dwight's cabinet was a member of SDS named Rich. He was a young white student with revolutionary politics and big heart and it was always nice to see and work with him. He was a leader in the anti-war movement and through his hands-on efforts, we were able to tap many of the university's resources. He was also instrumental in providing the white community with correct information in terms of what our movement was all about.

One day while Leonard and I were on campus, we were approached by a member of SDS and asked to meet with their members. A time was set up for later that night with the understanding that we would meet only with their key people. We listened as they explained their objectives and plans for action in Carbondale, and made arrangements for them to get 200 copies of the Black Panther Newspaper each week to sell along with their other information. Before we left, the one in charge asked to speak to me alone and we went into a room with a huge locker. He pulled out two shotguns, three thirty-thirty rifles and a thirty-eight six, all of which he gave us as a gift.

By this time our activities had become increasingly visible in the black community, as well as on campus. As a Black Student Union member I was able to set up tables in the university student center to do political education and sell the Panther newspaper. Headquarters in Chicago was sending us over 1,500 copies of the paper each week by way of the Illinois Central Railroad. The train traveled from Chicago to New Orleans making several stops including Carbondale.

One day while at the table in the student center a beautiful Black student named Kathy came up to me, looked me straight to the eyes and said, "I'll do anything I can that will help you." I gave her 50 copies of the Panther paper which she sold in less than two hours, came back and sat with me the rest of the day. She became one of my special support people in body and soul. A few weeks later a student named Blood from Yonkers, N.Y. came up to me and said he wanted to join with us because he knew one day there would be a showdown and he wanted to be there when it happened. I could tell from his demeanor he was interested in armed struggle and should things hit the fan, he would be there when it counted. That completed our crew; Leonard, Rab, Jimmy, Blood and myself.

## Taking Care of Business

Of all the points in the Black Panther Party Program, I always felt that Number 7, its call for organizing Black self-defense groups, was most important. We decided to train select members of Northeast Carbondale and select Black students in the safe and proper handling of firearms. We had located an abandoned salt mine approximately 10 miles from town which was isolated with many hills and slopes, ideal for Technical Equipment training (TE). We would never, in person or on the phone, refer to a weapon by the usual street term "piece." For us it was always TE.

The groups we trained were taught proper handling, loading and unloading and ways to improve accuracy for handguns, rifles and shotguns. We never practiced with these groups, we only taught. We did not want anyone to know our capabilities or techniques. The cadre practice sessions were completely different. We practiced standing, sitting, kneeling, rolling over then firing, running, steering a vehicle with the insides of our legs to free our hands and other techniques designed to maximize our effectiveness as a group. We all had Illinois gun cards, which were identifications cards with a picture and number that enables a resident of the state to purchase any firearms sold over the counter, that is, handguns, rifles and shotguns, as well as ammunition.

One day we were traveling from St. Louis, Missouri back to Carbondale, Illinois on Route 127. About 30 miles from Carbondale, just outside the town of Pinckneyville we passed a large white barn with a small sign painted in red which said "GUNS." We stopped the car and decided to go inside and see what kind of second-hand guns they were probably selling. I opened the door and to my amazement I saw wall-to-wall carpeting and elegant mahogany display cases full of every kind of handgun, rifle and shotgun imaginable. Nowadays there is a lot of talk about the 9mm handgun. However, 25 years ago the Browning 9mm, which holds 13 and one in the chamber, was our standard equipment well before most people even knew what 9mm was. We came back to the barn and bought seven 9mm and they became our main supplier, everything being strictly legit and legal. The store owner figured what we were about by our various choices of weapons, so every time we would make a purchase he would call the Carbondale Police Department and keep them abreast of our equipment. However, we had a friend who was a Black police officer, who used to keep us abreast of them keeping abreast of us.

As the demands of times were ever increasing I decided to move from the room I had and rent a three-bedroom house at 524 N. Wall Street, also on the northeast side. The house was directly across from the Crispus Attucks Park and elementary school. This house became home for Leonard, Rab, Blood and myself. Jimmy stayed with his lady and we felt it was better if we were not all in one location, while at the same time the house gave us even greater visibility in the community.

It was now early winter and clearly there was a need to expand the Free Breakfast Program from the Saturday program held in the Crispus Attucks School Cafeteria. For months I had attended church at the Mt. Olivet Freewill Baptist Church on north Marion Street. I knew it was important to attend a church in order to be further accepted by the community. One day I met with the pastor, Reverend Lloyd Sumner. I told him I wanted to start a Monday through Friday program to be located in the church basement. Rev. Sumner listened attentively and let me know he would speak to the deacons of the church and get back to me. When I spoke to him later in the week he said the deacons were all against it but he would give me the go-ahead anyway. Rev. Sumner said he would hold me responsible for the program and was giving his approval based on his faith in me. I know he was apprehensive but was supportive in spite of it.

Putting the program together was a phenomenal and demanding task. We were given the use of the basement but we had much to do to get ready. The strength, dedication and support from Blacks in the community and on campus are what ultimately made the program a resounding success. However, I had to first get in touch with Rich, student body vice-president, to let him know I needed to have an exterminator spray the Church basement to make sure there were no health code violations. Rich sent someone over the next day that took care of it.

The church provided us with all the cooking utensils needed to feed large numbers of people and also donated the use of electricity and gas I decided it was crucial to get the merchants of Carbondale to provide substantial amounts of food we needed through donations. I first went to the local A&P, spoke to the manager and explained what the program was about and what our needs were. A&P donated bread, butter, biscuits, grits and sausages on a regular basis. To this day I don't know how the manager did it but all the food he gave us was fresh. There were two other food markets including the local IGA who also made substantial donations.

In my contacts with these markets I either went alone or had a "sister" go with me so that there was no mistaken intimidation or appearance of a shakedown. New Era Dairy of Carbondale consistently donated crates of milk; we would just park our car in the back and load up. No money was ever exchanged. I'm going to right here, and now thank all of the beautiful people who through donations made this program possible. It was no small accomplishment that within a short period of time we were ready to roll. I must make one thing absolutely clear. It was the Black women from both the community and campus who stepped forward and ran the program. In order for the children to be fed in time for school it required that the women be at the church by 4:45 A.M. Many sisters volunteered to come in and cook on a regular basis. WE ALWAYS served a HOT breakfast—no chemically treated cold cereals. A schedule was put up and we never had a problem with help or no-shows. We were able to feed a surprising 150 children hot breakfast every morning, Monday through Friday. The program functioned with precision. The kids were fed and on line to leave by 7:30 A.M. There were so many children at the breakfast program that the school district was forced to send a bus to the church because the kids were not at the bus stop. This is a great example of how we impacted the community. Of all the things I've ever been involved in, the Free Breakfast for Children Program is the one I cherish the most. It demonstrated our love for the people and helped forge a bond between our movement and the community.

Along with our success and support in the community came increased surveillance of us by the Carbondale Police Department. However, we were in no way intimidated and they knew that. During November, I went to Chicago to confer with Fred Hampton and he asked me to set up a speaking engagement for him to come and speak at the university. I got in touch with Dwight and he arranged one of his staff to handle the speaking engagement funding. Universities provide X amount of dollars per school year to be used by student government to fund speaking engagements. I was able to get $1,500.00 for Fred to speak. This was a big move and I knew that security would have to be very tight. The date was set for November 14, 1969. The university student center, Ballroom A, on the second floor was reserved. We made arrangements for Fred, Bobby Rush, and others to go to a "safe house" upon arrival in Carbondale; safe house meaning a location not known by anyone that its occupants support our activities. When security measures were in place and all those attending inside the ballroom, Jimmy was to use the pay phone outside the ballroom and tell Fred to come on.

In order to secure the ballroom we had to search everyone for weapons. Jimmy and I did the male searches and Kathy did the female. Each person had to face me with arms extended I'd run both my hands down the right arm, then the left, put my hands behind the neck, up and down the back, then from the stomach to the chest with a pat under the arms. Then up the right leg to the crotch, up the left leg and also check all bags.

Fred arrived with five other members from the Chicago office. He came up to the microphone and the place rocked with applause. In the spirit of Malcolm, Fred began to speak. He talked about the needs of the people, programs of the Party, the type of individuals in the Black community that are in the way, the role of students and arm-chair revolutionaries. He spoke for about an hour-and-a-half and concluded to a standing ovation. Fred returned to a different house where he stayed until just before dawn, when he and the other members departed. The way that arrangement was handled; people knew we were for real.

A short three weeks later, I felt the same pain I experienced with the death of Malcolm. Fred was assassinated in Chicago in a house that he and other Party members occupied on Monroe Street two blocks from the Panther office. This brutal murder was part of the COUNTELPRO and was carried out by the Chicago Police Department with the full knowledge and support of the FBI. Using the cover of darkness, the operation was undetected because the police entered the alley behind the house in Illinois Bell telephone trucks and commenced to spray the house with machine gun fire at approximately 4:00 A.M.

Fred got on top of his wife Debra, who was pregnant, and shielded her and in so doing was brutally murdered along with another Panther, Mark Clark. In my mind the most important leader of the day was taken away. No one has been able to come close to Fred's ability to relate to the lumpen-proletariat, those below the working class.

Two days after the assassination we drove to Chicago and toured the house which was completely riddled with bullets. The house was open to the community and the lines were a block long as people continuously filed through the house for an eyewitness view of the blood and devastation. Police lying through their teeth, in the form of cocky Chicago States Attorney Hanrihan claimed it was a shootout. However, ballistic experts showed that out of all the bullets of which there were several hundred fired, only one cold have come from the inside.

Fred and Mark's lives were shortened because they stood up against oppression and were gunned down like public enemy #1. The federal government was in a state of open warfare against the Black Panther Party. Even with this being the case, we of the cadre, were not intimidated. We increased our organizing and most of the time getting only a couple hours sleep and even then, with someone awake at all times. All this was going on while I was still in school attending classes. Remarkably, I maintained a B average. I was able to do so by paying absolute attention in class, writing impromptu papers and going with what I had to the exams. There was absolutely no time to study. I enjoyed school very much but it was no longer a priority. Southern Illinois University had excellent facilities and a good faculty but school was no longer my reason for being in Carbondale. My primary objective was to organize the community and everything else became secondary. However, I remained active in the Black Student Union.

In February of 1970, Bill Cosby was invited to appear at the University as a performer/comedian. Bill agreed to meet with members of the Black Student Union at the Holiday Inn where he was staying prior to the performance. The meeting was scheduled in a conference room where there were approximately 20 students. A lot of small talk was going on when we of the crew arrived. One of the Black Student Union members said, "Bill do you have a message you would like to give to the Black Student Union?

Bill leaned back in his chair, pulled out this huge cigar and with this big grin said, "I make so much money that my income tax is over one million dollars." A feeling of disgust went through me. His response was all ego and had nothing to do with nothing. Crew members looked at each other and we headed to the door. With all the things we were dealing with we surely wouldn't waste time listening to anyone sitting around glorifying themselves.

That wasn't the only "notable" display by one of the most popular Blacks in America today. Jesse Jackson was invited a few months later for a speaking engagement. He arrived wearing a brown leather jacket, brown leather pants, and brown boots; sex appeal from head to toe. His ability to move a crowd was unquestionable, especially the ladies. When he was finished he was besieged by women with pen and paper asking not for his views but for his autograph.

## Cairo—The Not So Promised Land

Approximately fifty miles south of Carbondale is a town called Cairo, Illinois. In the 1800's Cairo was projected to be a city that would rival Chicago. It sits at the very southern tip of the state where the Mississippi and Ohio Rivers meet. In those days river and barge travel were considered No.1 in terms of commerce. The expectations for Cairo were very high. However, it never happened. It is a town in severe economic depression.

I remember my first visit there. Leaving Carbondale I took Route 13 east to Interstate 57 south. In less than an hour I arrived at the exit for Cairo and began the six miles south to the town limits. Right outside Cairo there were rows and rows of run-down shacks with a welcoming sign letting me know I had arrived at Future City, Illinois home of approximately 500 Black people. I was disgusted and angry. Here was a place without adequate sewer system and many residents using outhouses. This was 1969 not 1869. In order to understand the politics of the area take a closer look at the geography. Cairo sits 90 miles north of Blytheville, Arkansas and approximately 150 miles north of the Mississippi border.

The ways of the people and the politics are definitely of the south; no question about it. In addition there was a strong Ku Klux Klan and neo-Nazi presence in the area. As police brutality and racist terror took hold in the climate, the Black community responded by developing the United Front of Cairo, headed by Rev. Charles Koen, a young minister and Black activist. The United Front came together because Cairo was a community under siege by racists and neo-Nazi. During this period the national news carried reports of scattered racial incidents. However Cairo represents a city whose Black community was under violent attack for many years.

When I arrived in Cairo I was taken to the Pyramid Courts, one of the Black housing projects. These units were two stories, with two and three bedrooms. As we arrived at the projects I realized it was total darkness and no street lights on. Rev. Koen explained that the United Front shot out all the lights as a security measure due to the constant sniper attacks into the projects by the notorious White Hats. The White Hats were the Ku Klux Klan and neo-Nazis masquerading under a different name. The Chief of Police and the entire police force were all members. I went into many apartments where there were bullet holes in the walls. It was an obvious full-fledged campaign of terror. One of the White Hats favorite tactics was to use idle freight trains which were located along the back side of the projects and adjacent to the Mississippi River. The White Hats would fire into the projects from the freight trains with automatic weapons and then jump behind freight cars and disappear.

The United Front was a coalition of ministers and community residents and had the full support of the Black Community, both young and old. It was a spiritual movement, based in the church. There was singing of Black spirituals, picketing, demonstrations and other non-violent tactics. However, the United Front was no ordinary civil rights organizations. What separated it from the rest was its belief in armed self-defense. One of the slogans of the Front was draped on banners carried during demonstrations and read, "Before I'll be a Slave I'll be Buried in My Grave." A few times an article concerning Cairo did appear in the New York Times; however, no national televised news media featured Cairo with on-site coverage. This was no accident because to give Cairo the national attention it deserved would be to show the rest of the country and the world, that there was an American town under constant siege by racists and neo-Nazis and the Black community responded with continuous armed self-defense.

Reverend Koen requested my assistance in getting student support to aid the United Front in its struggle. Jimmy, Blood, Leonard, Rab and myself decided we would begin support in the following ways: Financial support through university speaking for Rev. Koen, soliciting donations from the anti-war movement, and when called on we would come to Cairo in a posture of armed self-defense, which we often did.

There were several exchanges of gunfire between us the White Hats. The constant sound of gunfire was often surreal. We also decided to help mobilize students to march in Cairo to protest the reign of terror against the Black community. I made a request for university buses and we had no trouble getting seven buses to transport 400 Black students to march with the people of Cairo. As a cadre we were never in favor of marches but made an exception for this one. Memories of Black people being brutalized and killed while marching was fresh in my mind. We came to the march with our 9mm's that we gave to the sisters we were dealing with, who walked with us while we served as marshals during the march. Of the 400 Black students who marched in Cairo approximately 300 were sisters (Black women). It was apparent that sisters were never hesitant to take a position on issues and back it up with action. However, several of the "brothers" at SIU talked a lot about Black power but were clearly intimidated at the prospect of facing off with the White Hats and neo-Nazis parading around with swastika arm bands. Sisters were the rock-bed of support throughout our presence in Carbondale and southern Illinois. Whether it was feeding us when hungry, letting us get an hour or two sleeps at their house while we were on the move or "watching our back" because sisters became just as proficient with a 9mm as we were. Although there are too many to mention by name, with these few words I salute all the sisters who never wavered in their faith in themselves nor their faith in us as we pressed forward through dangerous and uncharted ground. GOD BLESS YOU. I LOVE YOU.

Through our dedicated work several things became abundantly clear. Any Blacks who were on the front-line would be killed, jailed or compromised. Prisons provided and available source of individuals who were used by the federal COUNTELPRO program, as informers and planted in organizations to infiltrate and provide sensitive information used to target leaders in the Black Panther Party. Many convicted felons were recruited to infiltrate the Party through use of early parole. I remember during a political education meeting we held in Northeast Carbondale, a woman enrolled at SIU got overly friendly with Rab and was pushing herself on him. I was distrustful of her from the beginning and decided to check her story while Rab took her out one evening. Blood and I gained access to her apartment through opening her window. We went through all her personal belongings until we found letters that showed she had recently been released from prison and owed the state of Illinois $3000.00, which was a fine placed on her during sentencing for a felony conviction. After a while we didn't see her anymore. It is much easier to prevent individuals outside of a structure from penetrating, than it is to determine when someone you already have alliance with has been compromised.

## Time for a Set Up

The spring of 1970 showed a marked increase in the tension between the cadre and the Carbondale Police Department. Our residence at 524 N. Wall was under constant surveillance. The police engaged in practice runs on the house, converging from several directions and then driving by. We were not intimidated and accepted the fact that one day it would come to a show down. In the meantime the situation in Cairo had further deteriorated with the constant harassment and arrest of individuals in the United Front. The economic boycott of white merchants by the United Front was now a full year in effect. Cairo was a community at war and included helmeted policemen armed with sub-machine guns standing in front of stores during picketing and the National Guard poised on the outskirts of town. All of this was going on while our support and popularity in the Black community in Carbondale was at a very high level. It was out of this background that I was approached by two United Front staff members and told that because Cairo had become an armed camp, they had some equipment they needed temporarily stored. One such piece of equipment was an explosive device which they wanted me to hold for a few days. Explosives are equipment that the cadre and I were not interested in. Organizing the people and self-defense, yes, destructive activities of any kind, no. Being young, unfearful and in this case very unwise, I accepted the device and stored it in a closet. One of the sisters close to me would often say that I had no sense of danger. That was true. It was as if I expected to be a martyr or die as a freedom fighter and I accepted it as fate. I didn't realize I was being set up. On May 15, 1970 Rab, a sister and myself were in the house. At approximately 10:30 A.M. I went to the room where the device was stored, opened the closet with intentions of moving the device and it went off in my hand, rocking the house with a powerful explosion. I could feel myself lift off the floor heading toward the ceiling. I remember hearing Rab in another room scream, "Oh shit." Windows were blown out blocks away. The house was demolished. Remarkable, Rab and the sister though both wounded, were able to run out.

Rab, displaying extraordinary courage re-entered the structure and pulled me out on to the front lawn. I regained consciousness and I re-member laying there with half my leg blown off and blood everywhere. I lay there drifting in and out of consciousness, knowing I was dying. My internal body temperature felt like it was 300 degrees. The pain ripping through my body made me think that each of my arms and legs were tied to four horses and that I was being stretched out and pulled apart. I laid there saying, "God, I'm dying." A few minutes passed and a fire department emergency truck arrived and took me to Doctors Hospital. When I arrived at the emergency room, I looked up through a blur at several faces who began to ask questions all at the same time. I started to answer then realized this would sap my strength and I knew I was losing conscious but had the presence of mind to tell myself to start taking deep breaths so my system was working for itself when I went out. It was crucial that I stabilized my breathing in order to avoid going into shock. I went into a coma and remained in critical condition. It was a month before I opened my eyes and when I did my father was standing next to the hospital bed, had his hand on my forehead and a smile on his face. I was not expected to live and the doctor told my father that he would take his son home in a coffin. I had third degree burns over 70% of my body, severe loss of blood, smoke inhalation and gangrene which had set into my left leg and threatening to spread throughout my body. Anyone of these by itself could terminate my life. The sound from the explosion blew off parts of my eardrums; my father, a retired golf professional, was on the golf course in New York when he was summoned over the loud speaker to the club-house and given the news on the phone. It appeared on televised news that Reggie Brown, a Southern Illinois University student from New York had been critically injured in an explosion and had little to go on. My father got on a plane the next day, flew to St. Louis, Missouri and was met at the airport by Fast Eddie, one of the brothers from the northeast Carbondale and driven the 110 miles to Carbondale. They drove at speeds up to 90 mph. When my father arrived at the hospital it became evident that the doctors were less than cooperative. My father would have none of that and he let them know that if anything happened to me the whole hospital would be in jeopardy. My father, Charles Brown is a master in dealing with people and all business. When I opened my eyes coming out of the coma and saw him it gave me strength. He told me that when he arrived at the hospital I was almost completely burned but that within two weeks a crust had formed and miraculously came off leaving several small burns on my neck, chest and legs. Miraculously my hands were uninjured. I could not sit up nor barely talk.

I was getting a maximum shot of morphine every four hours around the clock. The pain would subside for about two hours and then for the next two hours a fight against hellacious pain to make it to the next shot. This was the case every day. I was in the isolation room in intensive care. There was the serious possibility of gangrene spreading through my body and require further surgery to stop it or death. My left leg below the knee was still wide open because the hospital did not have the equipment or the expert surgeons to operate and close the leg. One day, before my father arrived for his daily visit a white man in black colored minister's garb was allowed in my room. At first I thought he was a priest. I could not raise my head up but as he got closer I said to myself, "Oh no, this is serious trouble." He circled the bed and came to a stop along the bed, standing next to me. He had a scowl on his face, looked intelligent but very sinister. He leaned forward and a real sense of danger came over me as though my life might be taken. He raised his arm, pointed his finger and said "repent you ruthless sinner, you're not going to live, you're going to die and go to hell." My heart was beating fast and my breath got short. I pressed the call button for the nurse and called loudly for her to come. When the nurse arrived I told her to get him out of here for good. When my father arrived he was very angry and had it out with four of the nurses over the incident, I began to feel that the minister and the two United Front staff were somehow connected. No real minister would harass and intimidate someone close to death. What was his mission and who sent him?

Many people both black and white, were affected by the trauma that engulfed me. Cards and letters poured into the hospital. Sisters were especially sensitive to my suffering so much so that many of their cards and letters I still have. My will to live was very strong, while my recovery was slow and agonizing. There was the ever-present reality of the gangrene and what it could do at any point. My father stayed right on top of the doctors and they were forced to make appropriate medical decisions. An irrigation treatment was initiated to prevent the gangrene from spreading up my leg which would require further amputation of the leg, possibly all the way to the hip. I had to get out of bed and hold on to the side of the bed and with a nurse's assistance, lower my leg into a liquid solution. That was a real hell, since my leg was still wide open and the procedure had to be done once a day, every day. All the while, I was in critical condition but determined to live. I looked forward to my father coming to the hospital each day but was not allowed any other visitors. The doctors were uptight, the nurses were uptight, not wanting to give me their best but concerned about what the consequences would be if they didn't. I did very little sleeping and when I did I always woke up in pain. However the morphine was so strong that immediately following a shot, my skin would itch all over. There was a nurse on the night shift who told me if I needed another shot she would give it to me and that was a request I often made.

My father knew that eventually I would have to be moved from that hospital to one where additional surgery could be completed. What was about to occur was nothing less than an episode out of Mission Impossible. My dad planned to fly me out of Carbondale to New York in a private plane. What made it more intriguing was that the police wanted to question me and every day they posted a policeman outside the intensive care unit from 10:00 A.M. until midnight. My father convinced the hospital that it was in their best interests not to mention to anyone, including the police that we were leaving. The most crucial element was that the trip required a nurse and none of them were willing to go. Then Ms. Goodman, a nurse on during the day, told my father that if no one would go, she would make the trip. Ms. Godman displaying extraordinary courage risked her life and career. God bless you, I love you.

30

Utilizing the strong contacts he had made with physicians as a golf professional, my father had a bed reserved for me at the Hospital for Special Surgery, 70th Street and York Avenue, New York City, one of the best in the country and known for its surgery on professional athletes and the rich and famous. He also obtained the services of Dr. Marcove, one of the hospital's elite surgeons.

On a Thursday morning at the end of June we made our move. At 8:00 A.M. an ambulance pulled up to the hospital, I was wheeled out on a stretcher, still hooked up to the IV's and driven the six miles to the Southern Illinois airport. The airport is designed to only handle small aircraft. The ambulance drove directly onto the runway where a small propeller plan was waiting. My stretcher was loaded onto the plane and there was barely enough room for my father and Ms. Goodman. The pilot and co-pilot checked the controls and within five minutes we were in the air. My dad had pulled off a big one! It is an honor for me to carry his name. Getting the hospital administration to agree not to notify the police, and his ability to make the arrangements for the plane was accomplished in a community he was not familiar with and had been in only a short period of time. The ride was very bumpy and covered 1,100 miles from Carbondale to New York. Consequently, we had to refuel and did so in rural West Virginia, somewhere in Appalachia. The pilots, the nurse and my father all got out. As I lay on my back looking out the window a man in overalls approached the plane and said, "By golly there's a nigger on that plane and he must be some special nigger to have a white nurse traveling with him." I immediately heard my father say, "Get away from the plane." Obviously the man couldn't deal with seeing a young Black man getting specialized attention that required two white pilots, a white nurse and a private plane.

By the time we were in the air again, I was due for a shot of morphine which the nurse had to administer while we were going through a severe thunderstorm that continuously rocked the plane. Even though it seemed like an eternity we finally arrived at LaGuardia Airport and we were met immediately by ambulance which came out to the runway, just like clockwork. I was moved to the ambulance and we headed up the Grand Central Parkway to the Triboro Bridge. The bridge provides a magnificent view of the Manhattan skyline and this was the only time I viewed the skyline while lying on my back. We arrived at the hospital in 45 minutes. I was taken to the intensive care unit but was not placed in isolation because

31

the treatments had been successful in curtailing the gangrene. Of course my father was there throughout the day and when Dr. Marcove arrived I remember him telling my father that as long as I was not a member of the Weather Underground, that he would do the surgery. My father assured him that I was not involved with them and the surgery was scheduled.

The day after I arrived at the hospital my mother came to see me and as soon as she saw me she started crying. I could see the accumulated pain and sorrow of a mother whose son was near death and the emotional release of answered prayers, life. I was kept on the same medication regimen, however when the nurse gave me my injection of morphine it seemed stronger than what I got in Carbondale. I said to myself, hey that's cool, but as with all narcotics, the body builds up a certain tolerance, consequently the effect of a dosage does not remain the same. The day scheduled for my surgery arrived faster than I expected. All I could think of was that the closing of my leg would eliminate the pain and that I would begin to recover from my other wounds. After surgery I remember waking up in the recovery room with my mouth extremely dry and feeling totally dehydrated. The operation was a success, having been performed by one of the best in the business. I kept asking the nurse for water but she would take a small gauge pad, wet it and tell me to put it in m month. This I kept doing for three hours and it wasn't until evening that I received some fluids. What I immediately realized was that my leg and body was in the same amount of pain as before and it would be that way for quite a while due to the trauma and nerve damage that occurred. I was taken back to my room which I shared with another patient. The medication routine remained the same; one shot of morphine every four hours and two pills twice a day.

Then, one day disaster hit. I had received an injection at midnight and was asleep. Around 2:00 A.M. a nurse whom I had never seen before woke me up to give me medication. What stood out to me even while I was groggy was her appearance; tall, blond, and very sophisticated, something about her didn't seem right. She gave me pills I didn't recognize and at a time that I had not previously received medication. When I woke up I had an oxygen cup over my mouth and was connected to a heart monitor. The COUNTELPRO had struck. A Black nurse who worked the floor above me had taken an interest in my condition. I believe on her breaks she would come check on me, this particular time that she did, I was not breathing. She revived me and the first thing I heard her say was, "We almost lost you." The only people who knew where I was outside of my family and the ability to pull something like that off were the FBI. A case of J. Edgar Hoover gone mad, just like in the case of Fred Hampton and others.

The hospital told my father that one of my visitors gave me heroin and that I couldn't have any visitors outside of my parents. I think they really believed that however there were times when I felt that the hospital knew what happened and only took that position to cover itself. The hospital security had been breached big time. I was moved to a private room and given a nurse for each twelve hours. The next day the nurse that saved my life came to my room smiled, gave me a long stemmed red rose and left. I never saw her again. God sent me a beautiful guardian angel and I am eternally grateful. Wherever you are I hope there is utter peace and joy in your life and there will always be love in my heart for you. Later that day my doctor came to the room spoke to the nurse and then told me they were taking me off the morphine, cold turkey. Having recently come out of surgery and my wounds and leg still very painful, I was really shook up by his decision. For the first nine days my leg would be continuously jarred by pain that would lift my leg right up. My hands shook so severely that I couldn't hold a pen to write a letter. After the tenth day it was decided that I was well enough to go home. An application for Medicaid was submitted to the Department of Social Service and approved. With that accomplished the feds reappeared. The caseworker that approved my case received visits and calls at work and at home. She called my house and spoke to my father and told him that she was frightened. They would not focus that kind of attention on her unless it was part of a larger plan. In spite of all this I was still not intimidated. I needed all my energy to fully recover, get an artificial leg and learn how to walk again.

Having left the hospital in July, it was now August, I had my new leg, and at 22 years of age I started over taking my first steps. Learning to walk while in pain was a very difficult task. Once I received the leg I first had to learn how to walk while on crutches, and these I used until the end of September. I also found out that in early September, Columbia University had a program where if you scored high enough on a three hour exam, an individual would be considered for admittance to the university. I signed up for the exam, went to the lecture hall on crutches, handled the exam and was admitted to Columbia University. I knew I wasn't physically strong enough to attend at the time but would be ready the following year.

## *Seize the Time*

As a result of me being out of commission the cadre decided to broaden programming and activity in Carbondale. An NCCF (National committee to combat Fascism) office was opened on Washington Street on the northeast side. The office was fortified with sandbags and operated on very strict rules of security. A food Co-op Program was initiated where orders for meat were placed with the cadre; the orders were taken to a meat wholesaler out of town, enabling members of the community to purchase quality meats at a wholesale price. A Free Medical Program was started which was staffed with a doctor and nurse both young and white who volunteered their time three days a week providing the community with valuable clinical and medical services free of charge.

New members were brought into the cadre cell structure. In addition to LT, Rab, Jimmy and Blood, from Chicago came Doc, who was our medical person, having the ability to treat wounds and remove bullets. There was also House, a quiet no-nonsense urban guerilla, Fish our T.E. expert and repair person, and Gato, an intellectual from the university turned Panther. The cadre was completed with Joe a brother from northeast Carbondale, and Don whom and I nick-named A.B. because he was all business.

These brothers and the sisters who were with them represented what the Black Panther Party was about in its highest form and what Fred Hampton would have wanted and expected from us. What made the cadre special was its ability to relate to and not dictate to the community and thereby gain in strength through working with the people. Through having true love for Black people, the cadre was able to consider the needs of the people as the N0.1 priority and the needs of the Party as secondary. The fact that the community supported the cadre created tremendous anxiety for the Carbondale Police Department, who saw the cadre as a direct threat to their survival and were therefore in an actual state of undeclared war.

The atmosphere reached crisis proportions when Carbondale police officer, Larry Davis on patrol near the university an early October morning, 1970, was wounded by gunfire. An all-points bulletin went out for Jimmy who therefore fled the area. Since Jimmy was considered the perpetrator it was only a matter of time before open gunplay erupted. The cadre continued to maintain all the programs and especially the breakfast program because the most basic need of all people is food and the breakfast program remained a top priority in Carbondale.

At the cadre's living-quarters, 401 North Washington, around the clock surveillance by police intensified. It all came to a head on November 12, 1970 at approximately 3:00 A.M., when a university patrol car was hit by gunfire. Police claimed to trace a suspect to the area around 401 North Washington. Police vehicles began to converge on the area from all directions. Blood, who was awake on security, saw the first car as it arrived and he hollered, "pigs!"

It was never the intention of the cadre to defend a fixed location. Our intention was that if we were ever attacked to get out of the house, into the environment where our chances for survival would be greatly increased. It was also our policy to always have our shoes right next to the bed so that in case of having to leave on a moment's notice, we would not be wasting precious seconds looking for the other shoe.

401 North Washington was a two story house with all the bedrooms on the second floor. With shotgun in hand Gato was the first to jump out a rear bedroom window; next was Joe who also was armed with a shotgun. LT had one leg out the window when he felt bullets hit near his foot so he retreated into the house as everyone lay down and took positions at various windows. Gato and Joe were both hit by gunfire while trying to flee the encirclement. Gato was hit in the chest; Joe was shot in the back. That left L.T., House and Blood remaining in the house. Rab, Fish and Doc were out of town, while Don was at his lady's house. The police came armed with Smith & Wesson M79 Submachine guns. Thompson submachine guns, 30-30 rifles, 44 Magnum carbines, pump shotguns, other assorted weapons and tear gas. Police responded from the Carbondale Police Department, Southern Illinois University Police, Illinois State Police, Jackson County police and the police departments of Murphysboro and Marion, Illinois, some 20 miles away. Many police entered houses surrounding 401 North Washington, endangering the residents lives, firing their weapons from these vantage points knowing that the cadre would not shoot into these homes.

Blood, House and LT had several pump shotguns, 30-30 and Winchesters, 8mm rifles, Browning 9mm handguns and 45's. There were at least one hundred police taking part in the assault. First they would fire tear gas into the windows of the house and open fire on anyone coming to the windows to breathe. The cadre was equipped with gas masks and cement blocks were in front of the windows offering some protection from the gunfire ripping through the house. Both of these items proved to be key to their survival. L.T. House and Blood would rotate positions at different windows and at the count of three would rise up and open fire giving the impression that there were more people inside than it actually was.

Many people think that in numbers is strength, however, more importantly, in unity is strength.

Would it make a big difference if there were ten more people in the house? Not if their commitment toward each other was not true and complete. The result would be fear, chaos and death. True commitment and dedication makes an individual an army of one, a force to be reckoned with and recognized. To underscore the incredibleness of the cadre one need look no further than Don. During the shootout Don, who was in a different location, armed himself with a pump shotgun and Browning 9mm, and engaged police in gunfire in order to draw police manpower away from 401 North Washington.

If the cadre were a gang or a bunch of outlaws one would never find that level of commitment. For a true freedom fighter commitment is not negotiable. Consequently, knowing Don I was in no way surprised of his actions. I said to myself, "Yeah, that's Don." He was eventually captured and taken into custody. To most people I would say, who can you count on with absolute certainty to watch your back? Under pressure most people flee. As a matter of fact everyone will flee except those who represent unwavering commitment or unconditional love. The assault on the house went on until about 6:00 A.M., when residents of Northeast Carbondale came out of their houses and demanded the police stop shooting and allow the occupants to surrender. A half hour later House, Blood, L.T. emerged from the house to cheers from the community. Gato and Joe both seriously wounded earlier were rushed to the hospital as the others were taken into custody. The cadre's survival was no small feat considering the number of police taking part in the assault and the damage done to the house from the gunfire. The cadre members were charged with a 76 count indictment which included attempted murder, mob action, aggravated assault and criminal damage to property, the property being the police vehicles hit by gunfire. Total bail to get everyone out of jail would require over $175,000.00 cash. Many sisters from both the university and the community went consistently to Jackson County Jail to visit the cadre letting them know that when they got out of jail, the sisters would take care of their physical and spiritual needs. Miraculously, by the end of January all of the needed bail money had been raised, this was achieved in a small Midwestern town. The people's ability to raise and commit that amount of money represents the effectiveness of the programs created and maintained by the cadre. It was the Black community's way of saying that they and the cadre were one.

By the time the shootout occurred, I had progressed from using two crutches, to one crutch, to a cane which was quite an accomplishment for me, in being out of the hospital for only three months. By late January, with everyone out of jail, I decided it was time to get together with the full cadre and I made arrangements to fly to Chicago for a couple of weeks. When I arrived at O'Hare Airport I was met by Rab and driven to a safe-house apartment on the south side. Entering the apartment was a very gratifying experience. There was L.T., Blood, Jimmy, who was in hiding, along with Doc, House, Fish, Gato, don and Joe. The room was full of Black American freedom fighters, Gato and Joe were both fully recovered from their wounds. Blood had nerve damage in his hand from getting hit with a 44 magnum shell. Otherwise all was well. It was decided to stay out of Carbondale for a while and let things cool off. The decision was also made to put some distance between ourselves and the Black Panther Party because the national office had become very shaky. Huey Newton, co-founder and Minister of Defense was freed from jail due to overwhelming national and international support. Panthers and many others across the country were very happy with his release. The rank and file members of the New York office of the Party were eagerly awaiting Huey's planned visit to New York in order to see him and communicate with him. However, when Huey arrived in New York City he immediately went to Jane Fonda's central park west apartment, stayed there and upon leaving the city made no attempt to go up to Harlem and visit with the Panther brothers and sisters. That was a slap in the face and a big mistake. Huey was a living legend that became obsessed with the media hype and had no commitment to the rank and file members of Party. Eldridge Cleaver, the Minister of Information, fled the country and went to Algeria, on the run from a simple assault case, while Panthers across the country were facing various counts of attempted murder and other serious charges, and there was Eldridge, the Party's most visible spokesman running from an assault case. The Algerian government was very gracious. The Black Panther Party was allowed to establish an international section with a villa with use of equipment all at the courtesy of the Algerian government. After Eldridge fled the United States various members of the Party who were in leadership positions, showed up in Algeria pursuing their own selfish motives while deserting the heart and soul of the Party.

There are so many misconceptions about the Black Panther Party that very few people really know what the Party was all about. The misconceptions are due to a massive and effective smear campaign by the federal government, abandonment of commitment by Panther leadership and unfortunately a pervasive ignorance by many in the Black community regarding what a struggle for freedom entails. The FBI ran a constant smear campaign against the Party with accusations that 1) the Party was indoctrinating little kids into communists at the Free Breakfast Programs, a blatant lie. 2) the Party was a racist anti-white group causing fear among white Americans, where in fact we were strong allies for the anti-War movement and we received strong support from the movement, the Party was in no way racist. As a matter of fact, some of our strongest support nationally and internationally came from young white Americans and supporters of the anti-war movement in Europe. One cannot determine who to trust and level of commitment based on skin color. I have dealt with white people that I would trust with my life and I have dealt with some Black people that to trust would be dangerous to my health. It has nothing to do with race; it's all about what a person is made of.

When J. Edgar Hoover gave the O.K. to assassinate Panthers, federal and local law enforcement began to target Panthers around the country resulting in many assassinations and incarcerations the results of which there are Panthers who are still in jail today on trumped up charges. The average thinking Black person has no idea what a true struggle for freedom is all about. No people have ever marched their way to freedom. Marching is only one tool out of many in a struggle. From the American colonists to the Jews, to the Vietnamese, they all had to have their warriors to be successful, that is, the vanguard. Because of fear and ignorance many Black people want no part of that. They just want this "bad dream" to go away.

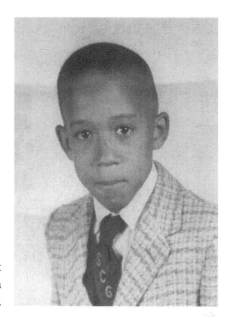

Me in second grade at
St. Catherine of Genoa
parochial school, 1956.

My loving mother
getting into a car,
1953. A legend in her
own time, she told
me the women on our
block used to wait
to see what she was
wearing before they
would start their day.

My mom, my dad, and a business associate. Before there was Tiger Woods, there was Charlie Brown, who taught three world champions how to play golf: Sugar Ray Robinson, middleweight world boxing champion; Joe Louis, heavyweight champion; and Althea Gibson, first black world champion tennis player, 1955.

My dad, boxing champion Sugar Ray Robinson, and his trainer, 1955.

My dad and me, 1990.

My mom and dad, 1990.

Me at a park in Harlem, 2005.

My wife, Monique, and me at a cookout, 2007.

My wife, Monique, 2011.

Carbondale
police officer
with a Thompson
submachine
gun during the
November 12, 1970,
shootout. Photo
courtesy of the
*Daily Egyptian*.

Community member Herb (*left*) and another community member (*right*) assisting cadre members during a negotiated surrender. Photo courtesy of the *Daily Egyptian*.

Community member speaking to Len, who came out on the ledge after his gas mask ran out. Photo courtesy of the *Daily Egyptian*.

Carbondale police taking cover just prior to surrender of the cadre. Photo courtesy of the *Daily Egyptian*.

Community members walking past the house shortly after the cadre surrendered. Photo courtesy of the *Daily Egyptian*.

With the Party leadership in disarray, we decided to do what was best for the cadre and that was to let us and the Party go our separate ways. Plans were made to go to Carbondale in February, 1971. We arrived in Carbondale and I decided to stay out of sight for at least two weeks. When I did surface many people in the community were amazed to the point of disbelief. Knowing how severe my injuries were they expected me to look totally messed up. However, the major burns to my body had miraculously healed and I looked virtually the same on the outside. That's one thing about physical wounds; no one can see the pain and anguish that simmers on the inside, much of which I did not understand until later in life. However, there was no time to focus on the changes I was going through. I was Reggie the organizer and cadre leader. Leadership gives an individual instant credibility. Outside of walking with a limp, I was virtually the same in everyone's eyes. To many I was a hero. The sisters in the community treated me with the kind of love and honor that only a few in life are fortunate enough to experience.

We used this time in Carbondale to go over with the lawyers some basic elements of the shootout. The lawyers came down from Chicago and were actively representing Party members there. When the shootout occurred they decided to become directly involved in the cadre's defense. Jeff, Mike and Flint are three young white lawyers, with hearts of gold and ability to match. It takes a lot of courage to come to a small southern Illinois town and represent Black Panther Party members in an attempted murder case of police officers. They were not intimidated and they came to take care of business. The states attorney of Jackson County was in no hurry to try the case because support of the cadre was very high on campus and in the community. Three days after the shootout hundreds of students, Black and White marched from the university to the house at 401 North Washington, where they toured the house and were able to see first-hand the hundreds of bullet holes that riddled the entire building. With that memory fresh in the minds of the community, the state's attorney felt it was best not to try the case until the spring of 1972.

One thing that holds true of college communities is, of course, that the student population is constantly changing. Whenever you return you miss some old faces and see many new ones. However, the non-student population remains relatively unchanged. 524 N. Wall and 401 N. Washington also remained visible, partially destroyed but visual testimony to be presence of freedom fighters. There had never occurred a case in the black movement where there was an exchange of gunfire with police and people in the movement, resulting in an acquittal through a jury trial. We knew that our task was formidable. Of course the possibility of going underground was discussed but it was our position that a political victory would have a very important impact on the Black community. Even though the odds were stacked against us we chose to stay and have our day in court. It was clear from the beginning that the defense of the cadre would require excellent preparation by the lawyers for there to be even a small chance of acquittal. What we had in our favor was that Mike, Jeff and Flint were better than good; they were genuinely interested in justice and were directly involved in social and political justice cases in Chicago. We knew it would be essential to have a jury of our peers, that, with significant black representation, and a large number of supporters at the trial. The states attorney again delayed the trial and had it put on the calendar for July because there would be fewer students in town. Nonetheless, we were prepared and "all systems go." We went throughout northeast Carbondale with a megaphone atop a car, informing the community of the start of the trial, asking for their presence and telling people where to go if they needed transportation to Jackson County Courthouse in Murphysboro. Three months earlier, Jimmy was taken into custody in Chicago in a case of mistaken identity. The police were looking for someone else when they surrounding him on the south side of Chicago. We knew we could call Jimmy to testify and Cook County would be required to transport Jimmy to Murphysboro, over 300 miles south.

When the prosecution opened its case it was with a parade of witnesses who were policemen involved in the shootout. Jeff and Mike did an excellent job cross–examining the witnesses and were able to get several officers to admit they fired first. When the defense presented its witnesses, they included many residents who lived in the immediate area of the shootout. These witnesses told how police forced their way into homes, took up positions and fired their weapons at 401 N. Washington, using the residents as shields and endangering the lives of all, young and old. The court was stunned by the testimony of a middle aged Black woman who spoke about how her husband worked nights and how her and all her children were exceptional in handling firearms and how she was always ready for trouble. So when the shootout started she rolled out of bed and hollered to her children, "get the guns y'all, get the guns," explaining she was ready to defend her family by any means necessary. Another woman testified how she and her children gathered on the bathroom floor as police, who forced their way into her home took up positions at windows and fired into 401 N. Washington knowing well that the cadre members would never fire into the homes of the community.

The defense then called L.T. House and Blood. We did not call Jimmy to testify as a cadre member, however, we just wanted him to get out of Cook County for a while and get a chance to see him. When Jimmy arrived the courthouse was packed with security, federal, state and local. There were police sharpshooters on the rooftops of many of the buildings surrounding the courthouse. Jimmy walked up the courthouse steps in shackles, no socks, sneakers with no shoelaces and a white pajama type outfit. The police were very worried that we were planning to make an attempt to free Jimmy, so they made sure his appearance would stand out and that he would end up bare footed.

One of the most important elements of the case was the physical evidence of the weapons taken out of 401 N. Washington. We smiled when all those weapons were brought in and put on display. However, every single rifle, shotgun and handgun was legally and correctly registered, which was crucial in a court of law. The trial lasted approximately four weeks. When the jury finally got the case my feelings swayed between confidence and grave apprehension. The jury contained three Blacks, all from Carbondale. The whites were all working people, one being the wife of a local car dealer we had done business with. On the day of the verdict there was incredible tension in the air. There were as many police in the courthouse as spectators. When the jury foreman began to read he counts for L.T., he started with the most serious charge first and said, "on the charge of attempted murder . . . not guilty." People jumped to their feet and roared their approval. The judge regained control of the courtroom and the jury foreman proceeded to announce all the counts of the indictment and the verdict was not guilty on all counts. The result was the same for each defendant. We were on a natural high. The prosecution was obviously bitterly disappointed. The jury concluded: 1) that the prosecution did not prove that the police officer shot near the university was in fact shot by an individual who went into 401 N. Washington. 2) Since the police did fire first and since all the cadre's weapons were legally registered, they were within their rights to defend themselves. This was the only case in Black history where a shootout occurred between police and Black people in the movement, gunfire exchanged, injuries on both sides and the defendants were acquitted of all charges, even the criminal damage to property charge (relating to the police cars that got shot up during the siege).

A few days later we went to the courthouse to claim our weapons. Imagine what it looked like and felt like for us to walk out of the courthouse and down the steps, guns in both hands. I thought to myself of the first look I had of the Party in 1967 on the steps of the State Capitol in Sacramento, California, with their guns in protest, realizing that we had taken the original principles of the Party and taken them to its highest level. The amount of political education that was provided by the shootout, trial and verdict is immeasurable in terms of its impact on the community. To see young Black freedom fighters take a stand and win in court is very significant. That is the most we could have hoped for in our commitment to organize and educate the community.

Jimmy's situation was however, unresolved. After the cadre's trial, the state's attorney got in touch with out lawyers and told them he was lowering Jimmy's bail on the attempted murder charge. It was the thinking of the state's attorney that if Jimmy got out on bail, he would flee and go underground and therefore he would not have to go to trial. Furthermore, he correctly concluded that with none of us incarcerated we would leave the area and move on. He was right on both counts. We had accomplished our goal in southern Illinois and it was now time to branch out. Most of us headed in separate directions and were able to tap into the network of people we knew and also remain in contact with each other.

## My Boss Cocaine

For three years I was a very active Black freedom fighter. When I returned to New York and my old neighborhood and I became Reggie from 156 Street. Many people in the neighborhood knew of my political involvement but only second hand. None had seen me in action. My support system became my old friends I grew up with, Billy Richard, Lonnie and several others. The neighborhood had changed dramatically in a few short years. Everyone was making crazy amounts of money selling heroin; this was during the French Connection days and heroin was everywhere. In 1973 I was still having a lot of difficulty with pain in my leg. Using the artificial leg began to wear down the skin causing breaks and wounds. In order to remain active I decided to medicate the pain with street drugs. First I tried sniffing heroin but didn't like it because it slowed me down. What I wanted was to be able to keep pace with the rest of society and not let my leg cause me to always have to walk behind others. Therefore, the heroin didn't serve the purpose. I began to hand out with friends who had contacts in the Hispanic community for cocaine. When I first tried it, the euphoria was unimaginable. I was alert, pain free and walking as fast as I wanted to. In my mind, it was the best of both worlds. I remember hanging with one of my friends who had people working for him selling heroin, when he invited me to ride with him to an afterhours spot in the Bronx called Featherbed. We arrived around midnight and inside were all these dealers from Harlem and fine looking young ladies. There was one dealer, Ice, who lived on my block before I went away to college. Now, he was a big time heroin dealer in central Harlem. He was wearing knuckle gold rings that covered each hand, way before it became vogue, the way it is today among some rap stars. Ice motioned with his head to a young lady and two of them rushed over like puppies vying for the attention of the owner. I said, "wow," so this is life in the drug world. We sniffed cocaine all night long and it never stopped flowing. My friend laughed at the numb look I had on my face because except for getting up to use the bathroom I was glued to the seat all night long sniffing and sniffing.

When we finally did leave I couldn't believe how much time had passed. It was now 1:00 P.M. in the afternoon. People were doing grocery shopping and laundry and there I was going home from the previous night. What was also interesting about that night is that it didn't cost me a dime. I was hanging with some young high rollers and I began to see big money makers getting younger and younger. One day at P.S. 28 playground two seventeen year old dealers pulled up, one in a BMW and the other in a Mercedes. They met to play some one on one basketball for cash. They asked me to hold the bet money but I was shocked when each of them handed me $500.00. It was as if they were saying welcome to the real world. It was around this time that I began to hang out with Lonnie, a childhood friend from 156 Street. He is the luckiest person I have ever known. It seemed as though he was always "hitting the number." He would play 605 every day, for no less than $5.00. Illegal number betting paid 600 to 1. So for a $5.00 hit you get $3000.00. It seemed as though 605 came out every month and sometimes twice in the same week, which really blew my mind.

In Harlem everything revolved around number playing and drugs. Many of my friends fell victim to heroin addiction. They would shoot up (main-line) and then just nod all day long. Sometimes you could see them standing on the corner and they would nod so low their head would almost touch their knees and then suddenly they would snap back up, only to nod out again. I didn't like heroin because it made people look ugly, nodding, their mouth hanging open and saliva dripping out. To me that was repulsive. However, cocaine did none of that. Those who had cocaine were held in high esteem on the street, especially by the ladies. Cocaine was much more expensive in the 1970's than it is now. What then cost $2000.00 for an ounce of cocaine now goes for less than half of that. In those days everyone would cut the cocaine, usually with inositol, a B vitamin. Today most people buy and sell it pure. During this period I seldom bought even small amounts of cocaine, instead purchasing powerful Colombian marihuana called "mota," which was also effective for pain. In 1973 I had two ear operations to close perforations in my eardrums caused by the explosion. I had the surgery at New York Hospital and while an out-patient I would periodically come in for examinations. One day I was sitting in a booth where the doctor had just put ear drops in my ear and momentary left.

While waiting for the doctor to return I swallowed and my whole throat was numb. I immediately thought of that night at the afterhours spot in the Bronx, where I sniffed cocaine all night long. I looked at the little brown bottle on the table and turned it around so I could read the label. It said cocaine 50% by volume. I said to myself, "hey what do we have here, liquid cocaine!" I got up and went to the next booth and it also had a bottle. I decided to take that one instead and returned to my seat. I never did ask why the ear, nose and throat clinic was using it or what it was supposed to do. All I knew was that it could get me high. I showed it to my friends who were dealing cocaine and they flipped over it. So, they would trade me $150.00 worth of powder cocaine for the liquid. For anyone sniffing large amounts of cocaine, the liquid was non-irritating to the nose. There I was trading hospital cocaine for street cocaine and therefore I always looked forward to my outpatient appointments.

In 1973 I resumed my education and enrolled in Columbia University for the fall semester. I enjoyed getting back in school and the challenge and prestige that went with attending one of the best schools in the country. For two years I maintained a B average and graduated in 1975 with a BA in political science. By this time I was spending my own money on cocaine, even though I was still hanging out with people making a lot of money selling drugs. What began to happen was that the more cocaine I consumed the more I could consume. That didn't bother me because I would just make a purchase get in my car and go to a girl's house or just cruise around Harlem and pick up a girl. The young ladies went for guys with a car and drugs. What cocaine allowed me to do was ignore my physical and emotional deficiencies. Even though I was handicapped I had cocaine and that meant I had girls. Emotionally, I had very low self-esteem due to tremendous difficulty in adjusting to being handicapped. I became self-conscious about the way I walked and would look at people as I walked down the street and I would automatically assume that they were looking at my walk and could tell I had an artificial leg. With cocaine, I didn't care what anyone thought and coke gave me influence, power and the ability to get women to do sexual favors and that's exactly what my friends were doing. Get some coke, pick up a girl and take her to the hotel that was the way it went. The real capable girls were called "freaky woo woo."

In the fall of 1974 I worked part time as a school aide at Brandeis High School and I really enjoyed that because some of the prettiest young ladies went to Brandeis. Little did I realize was that by this time I had become cocaine dependent. Cocaine was changing my behavior. I became less sensitive to my own needs and the needs of others. While working at Brandeis, I met a student named Angie who really liked me and all she wanted was for me to care about her. I would just call her and tell her I was parked in front of her projects at 100 Street and Amsterdam Avenue. I would just take her to the hotel and that's the way it went. My conversations with her were usually brief and never dealt with what her needs were, how she was doing or feeling. Time and time again I would just call her up and take her to the hotel.

When June 1975 came, the school term ended and so did my work at Brandeis, but I went back there for a visit in the fall. As I walked down the long hall I could see a young lady walking straight toward me, it was Angie. I said, "How you doing?" She wasn't smiling and just reached in her pocketbook and pulled out a picture of a little girl and said, "I want to show you a picture of your daughter." I looked at the pretty little girl in the white dress and made one of the biggest mistakes of my life saying, "how do you know it's mine?" She was hurt and disgusted but never raised her voice. She just put the picture in her purse and said "It's yours." Angie turned and walked away and I never saw her again. I thought my response was cool. It wasn't until years later that I began to feel the pain, sorry and pure anguish of knowing that I have got a daughter (now an adult) somewhere whom I want to tell her that I love her and I am here for her. Not a day goes by in my life that I don't think and pray about finding Angie and my daughter. I also want to ask Angie to somehow forgive me for never being there. My prayers and love go out to you Angie, a very strong Black woman, "I love you." Cocaine prevented me from being in touch with my feelings and it also changed my behavior even though I was not craving for it. By 1978 my social life was dependent on cocaine. As a member of the Black Panther Party I was committed to justice and positive change. When I began to self-medicate with coke, I did not recognize how I was using the drug to use women, something I would never have considered as a Panther. Cocaine is real insidious. It allows you to go along think you're an O.K. person. It had not changed how I looked but it was completely controlling my actions.

In 1978 I landed what was a dream job for me, working for American Airlines as a Reservation Sales Agent. By the time I had met my wife and had a three year old son. We were living in Mt. Vernon, New York when American Airlines called me on a Saturday afternoon and told me I would need to report to Hartford Connecticut the following Monday for processing. Then I had to be prepared to go to Dallas, Texas for three weeks of training. I knew the job would require that I relocate to Hartford but I didn't care. I only thought of all the free travel that would be available and the prestige that went along with it. Being able to tell people I work for American Airlines compensated for my low self-esteem due to my injuries.

American Airlines has one of the most professional and extensive training programs in the airline industry. Training is designed to weed out any new employees who can't handle pressure. For example, when I arrived in Dallas I was given general information, my room and a tour of the facility, which is halfway between Dallas and Fort Worth, Texas My training schedule was 11:00 P.M. until 7:00 A.M. and then two additional hours in the afternoon. Doing training in the middle of the night was very intimidating and designed to separate the strong from the weak. Many people would leave after the first week because it was too much pressure. I completed training and went home for one week before getting ready to head to Hartford.

It took me no more than a month to realize that I didn't like the place. To me it was just a conservative New England town. So what if it was the insurance capital of the U.S. it didn't have any appeal to me and I knew I definitely wasn't bringing my family there. In spite of that, I was able to work in Hartford for three years. The travel incentives and overtime money kept me going for a while. At the time airline employees could rent a car from Hertz or Avis for $7.00 a day with unlimited mileage. The car rental companies gave airline employees that deal because airlines generate car rental business. I would drive home every weekend with a different car. When I went to my old neighborhood people would see me with all these different cars with Connecticut license plates and they thought I had made it big in drugs, when actually was just doing drugs. After three years I resigned from the job because I didn't want to stay in Hartford. I tried commuting from Mt. Vernon and that lasted seven months before I resigned.

It was now 1981 and I was looking for work and quickly found it. Another of my friends from 156 Street had also made it big. Douglas was selling cocaine and marihuana on a small time basis. Then one day all that changed. Operating out of a north Bronx apartment he was approached by a Dominican girl who lived in his building and asked for his help. One of her brothers was very sick in the hospital and the family did not speak English very well. They felt the hospital was jerking them around due to the language difficulty and there was fear he might die. Douglas went to the hospital and stayed most of two days. He talked to the doctors and kept the family informed as to what was going on. The young man's condition improved and the family was very appreciative. Douglas did not know they were well connected but they knew he was selling cocaine. To show their appreciation they gave him a kilo of cocaine on consignment and Douglas never looked back.

Doug knew my political history and felt I was trustworthy. When we were growing up our buildings faced each other and we never got into any serious fights or beefs. So, he made me an offer I didn't refuse. He would pay me $600.00 a week and a quarter ounce of cocaine to answer the door and drive the car when necessary. I would also get to sniff cocaine every night after work, six days a week. I said, "no problem." I had seen a couple of ounces of cocaine before but I couldn't believe what a kilo looked like. I used to call it the grape juice because when you opened the zip lock bag a strong aroma similar to Welch's grape juice would fill up the whole room. Douglas was now connected to people who were bringing it in the country. I thought I had it made, getting paid well to work security six days a week, no working on Sunday.

One of Douglas' best customers was a retired player for the New York Knicks who would bring current NBA players to Douglas when they were in town playing the Knicks. Our rule was that they had to come after 1:00 A.M. so that none of the other customers would see them coming and going. We didn't do any regular business after midnight. When you have people ringing your bell at 3:00 A.M. and 4:00 A.M. neighbors are much less tolerant of how you make your living. We also would not deal with anyone who did not call before they came. Human nature suggests that if someone knows your phone number but comes by your house unexpectedly, they intend to catch you unprepared and gain the advantage in the situation. I also found that people were quick to use the presence of women to get the best deal possible. Men would bring young ladies with them because they were a distraction and can also soften you up to get a better deal.

One thing about this business is that you never know when someone will attempt to "take you off." Many apartment buildings in New York City have what's called dumb-waiters, which are garbage disposal compartments in each apartment made into the kitchen wall. You simply open the compartment door, place the garbage on the platform operating like an elevator, and the garbage would go down to the basement. Dumb-waiters have not been used regularly since the late 1950's and in most buildings they are sealed and locked. One of our customer's fathers was a superintendent of a building and the customer therefore knew about the workings of the dumbwaiter system. He got his girlfriend to enter the dumbwaiter from the roof, lower it to our fifth floor apartment and force open the door using tools while inside the dumbwaiter. Being in a rush and an addict, she grabbed the first thing she saw; which was, two pounds of marihuana, but on the same closet shelf was $20,000.00 in cash.

When we arrived at the apartment later in the day, we both had a look of disbelief. We were told by a young lady who lived next door what had happened. After that incident I found myself getting very paranoid. When alone in the apartment and sniffing cocaine, I would put my ear to the wall, listening and wondering whether there would be further surprises. I was using cocaine heavily and whenever I went to work I was always preparing myself for and expecting the worst. I had become very unhappy and still could not see that I was addicted.

In some ways it's amazing, most people have to go and look for drugs, however drugs have always been readily available and unfortunately a big part of my life. I knew sooner or later something had to give. I told Douglas that I felt that the DEA or TNT would soon be coming through the door. He laughed in disbelief but that didn't bother me. I told him I would work until the end of the week and then I'm out. I gathered my family and fled New York because I felt that if I stayed I would end up going to jail for a very long time. I went back to Illinois and enrolled in Southern Illinois University taking some graduate courses while my wife went to undergraduate school. Well, moving over 1,000 miles really didn't change much because I was still willing to flirt with disaster. I made contact with Douglas who ironically had taken my advice. A week after I left New York, Douglas packed up and moved the operation to Riverside Drive in Manhattan. Wouldn't you know, three days after he moved, the NYPD, Tactical Narcotics Team busted through the door only to find an empty apartment?

While back at Southern Illinois University, one day I was working out in the weight room and met Big Al, a young white guy who was an extremely powerful weightlifter. I don't think I ever saw anyone bigger or stronger than him. Well Al and I frequently talked and he eventually let me know that he was selling cocaine, however, the quality he was getting and the price he was paying was no match for what I could get him back in New York. To my surprise Al called me to his house and told me he would let me do deals for him. Big Al was ready to get busy and he gave me an envelope with $15,000.00 in one hundred dollar bills and a credit card to cover the gas and any expenses. He told me he would give me $500.00 when I returned.

I was going to negotiate for more money but didn't because Doug told me he would give me two ounces of cocaine for each deal. I had an arrangement where I was getting paid on both ends. I made the first trip and it went over without a hitch. My beautiful wife, at my request, prepared food for me to make the trip. I had fried chicken, cold cuts, carrots, crackers, and two gallons of juice and a gallon of water. It was 2, 2000 miles round trip and I only stopped for gas. As a matter of fact I got an idea that I would bring my jump rope and whenever I stopped for gas I would do 200 jumps to increase my cardiovascular and circulation and it definitely helped. I did get tired but not very sleepy. Obviously, Al was pleased when I returned with his goods; therefore the first trip was just the beginning.

I heard somewhere that a little paranoia is good for you; well, I do believe that. At any rate I immediately made changes in my MO (mode of operation). I made many trips to New York and I never did any of them exactly alike. I told Al when he would hand me the money for the product that I would see him within 4 to 5 days. Sometimes I would depart 30 minutes after leaving his place and other times I would leave the next day. I would never tell him the exact day that I was coming back, in order to protect my own security. I would call Douglas; let him know I was on my way to New York City and that I would see him at a certain hour. Well, Doug was truly fascinated that if I told him I would be there at 7:00 P.M. and would be ringing his bell before 7:30 P.M. He found it unbelievable that I could travel 1,100 miles alone and arrive within 30 minutes of my expected time.

All of my trips did not go quite so smooth. Sometimes I would decide to fly out of St. Louis to NYC, therefore I would have to drive 110 miles from Carbondale to Lambert Field, park my car and jump on a plane. On one particular trip I scheduled myself on a 7:00 A.M. flight, which meant I would need to leave Carbondale at approximately 4:00 A.M. Well, about an hour into the car ride I had to pull over to relieve myself. Unfortunately, the car was in soft grass so when I got back in the car the wheels just spun around and went deeper into the ground. There I was on rural route 127 in the middle of farmland and coyotes when after about 20 minutes a man in a pickup truck rode by, turned around and came back. He got a chain out of his truck and pulled my car out of the grass. I offered him $20.00 but he steadfastly refused to accept it. Some people in this country really have character. It did not matter that he was white and I was black and he wasn't interested in inviting me to dinner. He stopped because it was a tradition and that was what he was taught to do and that's what he'll always do regardless whether it's 4:00 A.M. or 4:00 P.M.

That delay did not make me miss my flight but it should have served as a warning to me. Well, I arrived in New York, picked up the package and sniffed cocaine until the next morning at which time I took a cab to the airport. One thing has always been apparent to me. Drug enforcement agencies and police departments all have profiles of drug users and couriers. So if you want trouble wear a lot of gold, sneakers and your cap on backward. Well, I arrived at the airport in a three piece suit, and overcoat from F.R. Tripler, Madison Avenue, with matching hat. Actually I had a half kilo of cocaine in two envelopes in my coat and inside suit pockets. I went through the metal detector and it went off.

Did airport personnel rush over to me? No. The security calmly but firmly asked me if I had any keys or coins in my pockets. Yes, I did and placed them in the cup and went through the metal detector again, this time without incidence. I boarded the plane and flew to St. Louis. On my way back to Carbondale I got stopped for speeding and when I was pulled over I had the product in my overcoat on the back seat. The state trooper issued me the speeding ticket and let me go on my way.

There is one other incident I must relate. Once I drove up to New York and picked up a package and while returning to Carbondale I decided I would make a stop in Dayton, Ohio. Well I'm driving along I-70 extremely high off cocaine and I decide to go see a couple young ladies I met that live in Dayton.

Well, I had only been to their house once and they lived in the housing projects. When I got to Dayton I couldn't find the residence because there were at least three different developments and all the projects looked alike. I'm persistent, so I keep looking only to make a turn down a one way street, going the wrong way. In an instance blue lights are flashing. Yep, it's the police, right behind me.

My heart is racing and I'm wired. I tell myself to relax and close those eyes a little, as I know they are wide open due to the coke. I take deep breaths as the police officer approaches and I role down my window. "Driver's license and registration," says the officer. Instinctively I told myself; give him more than what he asked for. I hand him my driver's license, registration, and my university identification card. I figure that will lessen suspicion and give me some credibility.

He tells me that I went down a one way street the wrong way. I explained to the officer that I am returning to school from New York and I was getting sleepy behind the wheel so I got off I-70 in Dayton to go to a friend's house to sleep for the night and that I was having trouble locating the residence. I learned that whatever you say to police when stopped, your core statement better be based on truth. Yes, I had just come from New York and yes I was returning to Illinois. If you concoct a complete lie and it doesn't hold up you are definitely going to get searched on the spot and taken to the station. The officer took my license, registration and I.D. and returned to his car.

As a rule I always position my side mirrors and rear view mirror so that I never have to tilt or move my head. All I did was sit completely straight but my eyes occasionally moved from mirror to mirror. For over 30 minutes I sat completely still, never leaning forward or reaching for anything. Any movement you make in a car is considered "probable cause" and can justify a search or worse. There I sat, my life flashing before me contemplating doing big time in the Ohio State Penitentiary. I also thought of my wife and kids, wondering if I would ever see them again. What I feared most was the arrival of another patrol car. None came, so I still had a small ray of hope.

Now is the moment of truth. The officer finally opened his patrol car and slowly walked to my car. Those five seconds were among the most agonizing in my entire life. He looked down at me, I looked up at him. He said, "I'm going to show you how to get back on the highway," and he handed me my I.D. Those words were sweet music to my ears. There I was with out-of-state license plates, pulled over on a one-way street going the wrong way, with a half kilo in the trunk and I drove off without even a traffic ticket. God is surely merciful! That's why I praise Him, all of the time. My shrewdness helped a tiny bit but it was God that got me out of that jam as He does for me time and time again; little jams and big ones too. I pray I will grow to do His will before He puts my lights out.

With all this constant drug involvement, it wasn't before long that I was introduced to what became my worst nightmare, free basing (smoking) cocaine, instant high and instant trouble. My life began to slip away. By this time I had two additional children. To make matters worse, my oldest son was diagnosed as developmentally disabled which meant he needed a very structured environment at home, which I was doing nothing to provide. I had failed myself and my family. All I wanted was to get high. I began to spend time with lowlifes. I became a low life. You can dress well and keep an excellent appearance and still be nothing but a low life. What make you a low life is your actions. I had cocaine but that was all I had. My behavior had changed drastically but I still couldn't see it. In the beginning I thought my association with "the boss" would be a short-term temporary thing. Little did I expect to work several years just to be with the boss as much as possible? No matter where I worked or what job I had, my boss was still the same . . . cocaine. People like to say that a person will change when they hit rock bottom. I disagree. There's no such thing as rock bottom, because what you perceive as rock bottom can get even worse. When adversity is present in a person's life one of the first things you hear is "Oh my God." Well I said that a lot too. I wanted out but wanting and doing are often not the same thing.

---

## Recovery

Cunning, baffling and powerful, these are some of the words used to describe cocaine. No matter how bad your life gets and how many loses you suffer the drug can remain as alluring as ever. There is often the thought that "a hit" would feel real good right about now. I had lost or left many jobs and spiritually abandoned my family nevertheless the temptation remained, though sometimes dormant. Sooner or later getting treatment becomes a matter of life or death. I always thought I could manage the drug and get high in a so-called responsible manner. Very rarely have I used cocaine responsibly and more often than not my family has suffered consequences every time I used. When I used to think of the word abandon, I thought of a car being left on the side of a road, or an infant being left in a hospital or sailors abandoning ship. I now have a clearer understanding of abandonment and the devastation it reaps on families headed by cocaine and crack users. Through my cocaine use I abandoned ship and left my wife and children to fend for themselves. This was done through spending consecutive days and nights away from home while using cocaine, coming home totally broke and missing family plans, outings and important business. Even so, I would spend the next day eating well and being concerned with how I looked on the outside while my inner spirit was being dealt a death blow. My children began to ignore me, acting as if I wasn't there. I would call them two or three times to get them to respond. Eventually my nine year old daughter and eleven year old son began to argue about everything and I falsely concluded this was sibling rivalry. Little did I realize they were responding to the arguing my wife and I had as she desperately tried to hold the family together. My wife realized she was codependent and needed therapy because of my drug use even though she never used. I had taken her for granted all those years and was therefore unable to see the importance of the fact that she had begun to see a therapist as an outpatient. I concluded that it was good for her to see a therapist to help her cope, not realizing she was taking serious steps to totally cut me out of the picture. Nero and I have a lot in common. We both fiddled while our foundations burned to the ground. My life was fading fast. I had heard the word recovery so often but I never knew what it really was. Right in the middle of recovery is the word over. Old attitudes and behaviors are out and the willingness to go to any length to maintain sobriety is in. Recovery also means a rebirth of the spiritual self which was miserably abandoned in addiction by me. I realized I needed to go away for treatment and began to pray for guidance from God. It has been revealed to me that often God gives me answers not in my own mind but through the positive people who are around me and care about me and therefore expressing God's love for me. One of my wife's friends worked in a detox unit in the local hospital and had referred people to a drug treatment facility in south Florida. She suggested I call them, talk to the director and decide what I wanted to do. I always wanted to spend some time in Florida but never expected it would be while in treatment. I used no cocaine or crack for three weeks prior to making arrangements to enter treatment. I found out on the phone that the average length of stay in treatment at this program was three months but could be longer or shorter depending on your individual treatment plan. I gave my kids hugs and kisses before they went to school and my wife drove me to New York City to catch a flight to Palm Beach Airport. I prayed to God for a safe flight and in less than three hours I was in Florida.

The Palm Beach airport is beautiful. You can tell when you are in a vacation airport because the pay phones have buttons you can press for the hotels and rental car agencies, no dialing is necessary.

The facility is about thirty miles from the airport and there's nothing like rows and rows of palm trees to make you feel like things won't be so bad. Drug treatment is big business with millions and millions of dollars at stake. Having worked in human services, I've seen many programs that are in it just for the money and will even fabricate documentation of individual counseling sessions in order to increase revenue and maintain state and federal certification. It didn't take long to find out that Renaissance Institute, the program I chose, was for real. You are busy from

9:00 A.M. until 9:00 P.M.; no fluff or bull just extensive and professional treatment. I thought everything would fit right in place but little did I realize how much work I would need to do on myself.

Having used drugs so many years I was able to suppress all my anger and rage. I had no idea how angry I was until I began to experience my anger in treatment. I was angry about being set up as a Panther, angry about being an amputee and had a real bad temper, especially regarding anything I concluded had racial overtones to it. Most of this was hidden from me through using cocaine. The clinical staff concluded that for me to maintain my sobriety it would be best for me to remain in Florida awhile after completing treatment. Initially, I was very reluctant to even consider it. I was anxious to get back to my wife and attempt to make amends to her and spend a lot of time with my children. I was undecided as to what I would do but realized I had to make a decision over the weekend of my seventh week in treatment.

Renaissance wanted me to make a commitment. Sunday morning I attended the sunrise Alcoholics Anonymous meeting at the beach, a very beautiful experience. People in recovery, young and old, rich and working class, meet just before sunrise and form a circle and share feelings. The sun rises over the ocean, pelican's fish for food and one can hear the peaceful sound of waves hitting the shore.

After the meeting I was told by someone to pray for willingness, that is, the willingness to go to any length to maintain sobriety. I knew I wasn't spiritually ready to return to New York so I put my faith and trust in the program.

Essential to any recovery is the commitment to change the people, places and things frequented in addiction (while using drugs). The ability to let go and focus on life one day at a time keeps me from picking up a drink or a drug. One day my therapist told me that she had a drug dream the night before and she was someone who had been clean for over ten years. Yes, it is cunning; baffling and powerful. Many people come into treatment expecting the program to fix them while they just sit back and take it in. Recovery comes from working on your character defects: anger, fear, resentment, dishonesty, manipulation, ego, lying, stealing, gossip, judging others, low self-esteem etc. God helps those who help themselves is so true. "God grant me the serenity to accept the things I cannot change, the courage to change the things I can and the wisdom to know the difference."

The serenity prayer is a very powerful statement and the key principle is acceptance. Who among us truly accept the things about us that we cannot change? I learned while in treatment that I didn't truly accept being an amputee. In all the years since losing my leg I never considered functioning in the community with my leg off, using crutches. Even though I was often in pain and my stump very sore, I refused to allow myself to stand out. I would put my leg on and if I limped, so be it. I did not want to be physically vulnerable and I did not want any stares or curious looks. I did not accept the reality that I am an amputee. Consequently, I always kept my leg on except when sleeping or bathing. I blend in well by walking with as little limp as possible. I was not O.K. with being me. While in treatment my therapist suggested I do two things that I completely refused to consider during my twenty years as an amputee.

First, was to take my leg off and get in the swimming pool. Even though treatment is a spiritually and physically safe environment, I felt very uncomfortable walking out to the pool on crutches with my leg off. I sat on the edge of the pool hopped in and began to swim a couple of laps. Previously I had fear of whether I would drown or look bad but it was all unfounded. The second task was to keep my leg off the days I didn't work and instead use crutches getting in and out of the van and going to meetings in the community.

Well, I had not been in public with my leg off since I came home from the hospital so I was somewhat hesitant. However, I was determined to work on my willingness and I therefore followed the request. It is amazing that many of the things we hold on to for years that are blocking our wellness and happiness can be eliminated in an instance by having the will and love of self, regardless of what anyone might say or think.

However that was only the beginning, a small step on a long journey. The disease of addiction is forever, how you deal with it is up to you. You either get sober or you die, sometimes quickly, sometimes slowly. Many people, including myself, often feel we can do it our way. When we do, right around the corner is the pain of a lost relationship or job etc., and we're right back to using. I'll never forget that while I was in Florida after coming out of treatment my wife notified me that she was filing for divorce. I was working as a lab secretary at a local hospital during which time I met a beautiful black young lady. She was stunning, actually gorgeous and with a warm and beautiful personality. We would go for walks on the beach both day and night and often just open sun roof and cruise. Due to my divorce I was afraid to be alone, I didn't want to be alone, and therefore, my relationship with this young lady received all my attention . . . bad move. One evening we made plans to go shopping Saturday morning. I had about $800.00 and I was going to buy her and her little girl something nice and also a little something for myself and just chill.

Well, Saturday morning came and I'm waiting for her phone call. Several hours pass and it's now afternoon. I called her several times but got no answer. By now I'm hurt, actually devastated. A feeling of total abandonment overwhelmed me. My recovery was already on shaky ground because a month earlier I began a "marihuana maintenance program," smoking weed on a regular basis. However, when I heard nothing from my friend, it wasn't marihuana that was on my mind. I put my money in my pocket, walked out into the Delray Beach sun and I knew exactly what I was looking for. Part of the madness about addiction is the fact that one develops keen insight into who you can approach to get drugs. Even if they don't use you can often tell who it's cool to approach about where to get it. A car pulled into the gas station and I knew right away that this was the one. I asked the occupants to take me to get some crack and that I would fill up their gas tank. They took me to the other side of town, you know, the Black side, went and got $20.00 of crack, brought it back to the car with something to smoke it in. I lit it up in the car which immediately opened the door to hell. I went inside the crack house and began smoking non-stop. After a couple hours a guy who was also in the house was sitting right across from me when he began to have a heart attack. EMS was called, so I had to gather up my rocks and go outside, which I hated. Very few people like to be outside while high. Anyway, after the ambulance left the residence I went back in. An hour passed and guess who's at the door, the guy who just left in the ambulance, coming back to smoke some more. Unreal!

I stayed in that house until the following morning. When I got back to my apartment I didn't have a dime in my pocket and was full of utter depression. The phone rings and it's my friend saying she had been trying to get in touch with me since yesterday. She explained that she didn't get in touch with me early Saturday because of a medical emergency regarding her grandmother. When I told her what I had done she was devastated. She immediately put distance between me and herself, keeping her answering machine on and eventually changing her phone number. That whole episode was a crushing blow to me. I lost my recovery, my friend and was on my way back to New York to handle divorce.

Therapists will tell you time and time again to keep the focus on yourself, keep your recovery first. I wasn't ready for that relationship because I wasn't well. First moment of doubt and I ran and got high.

I've since learned after many struggles the true meaning of the words: "To thine own self be true." As human beings we all have issues with or without drugs. However, using drugs ad or alcohol pretty much puts resolving our other issues or character flaws completely out of reach. As I began a real program of recovery, slogans I heard a thousand times began to take on new meaning. "One day at a time." Well, it's true, my life is really just one day at a time and as long as I stay focused in today, not dwelling on the past, or what I had, nor worrying about the future, then, everything really is OK.

I'm still living and breathing through the grace of God, taking care of business and giving my children and loved ones unconditional love. I've got a life and a sense that there are better days ahead.

## Take a Look

One thing about recovery, you can live it but you can't live without it. It is an opportunity to start life over. One doesn't make up for lost time; we merely have today, this moment. The past is over but one must surely learn from it and use the past to become better. Better for me is not just recovering from addiction but being better equipped to fight the good fight of faith and the fight for justice. Justice is an issue regarding many people that are discriminated against due to race, ethnic background, physical handicap, mental retardation, mental illness, behavior disorder or even gender.

The constant among all of these conditions is that they require the presence and commitment of advocates to ensure justice and empowerment. I have worked with a variety of populations and will continue to work on their behalf. At the same time I see the needs of Black people becoming more acute. Racial hostility, Black youth without leaders or role models, single Black women raising families, staggering numbers of Black children in foster care awaiting and in need of adoption, are all part of the crisis in Black America.

The renewed notoriety of the KKK prompts many to declare that the Klan is back in business. Actually they never stopped doing business. There are many white hate groups and militias that are well equipped to get their message across and engage in violence if the case may be. Black people need to wake up and smell the smoke. Where is the Black leadership? There is no real Black leadership.

Who is really for real? How about Black Republicans? Take a close look at any Black person that's a member of the Republican Party. Republicans have historically cut the funds for Head Start, aid to the elderly, programs serving the disabled and are obviously and openly anti-Black on issues affecting the Black community.

Let's look at the pathetic state of Black youth. They are into rap but what else are many of them in to? Unfortunately, violent robberies, gangs, murder and selling drugs, while less and less of their numbers are finishing high school. Obviously, the most serious crisis in the Black community is the plight of Black youth. So where are the role models? Where are mom and dad? As a matter of act, where is dad? Two thirds of all Black children are born into homes headed by single Black women. Where are those guys? So many black men still have the Mandingo complex and are unfortunately and scandalously functioning mainly as breeders. A father is biological; a parent is your role in the family. Most Black fathers are not a parent but they've fathered children all over the place. Consequently, for many Black youth the family portrayed in the Cosby show is like a comic strip; it is so far removed from their life experiences.

The road for single Black women with children is very difficult, especially raising boys. In Black communities across America the gang mentality is on the rise among Black male teenagers with many of them heavily armed. The Black man must step forward. When you bring children into the world, you are responsible for their mental, physical and spiritual growth. It does not matter whether you are married, nor does it matter which woman you live with. You must be a role model to your children wherever they are. Therefore, make a commitment to spend time with all your children and do it often.

In New York City alone there are over 20,000 Black children in foster care in need of adoption. There is genocide going on and crack is the culprit. It has the power to wipe out a whole generation of people. Furthermore, addicts abuse and neglect their children. You hear a lot about abuse but what about neglect? A neglected child is a child less than 18 years old whose physical, mental and emotional condition has been impaired as a result of the failure of his or her parents to exercise a minimum degree of care. Crack-heads are incapable of supplying the child with adequate food, shelter or clothing.

Addicts would be more likely to use excessive corporal punishment and by using drugs or alcohol are more likely to lose control of his or her actions. Many kids in foster care have been completely abandoned. Kids are left on the street, with other people and many times left in the apartment with the parent never returning or returning days or weeks later.

I attended a North American Conference on Adoptable children in Atlanta, which hosted many professionals and parents involved in adoption. I remember seeing at one of the workshops, a white woman with a Black infant that she had adopted. For those Black people who don't like the idea of white people adopting Black children, then why don't you adopt? These children need loving homes and if white parents or any other parents provide, then it receives 100% of my support, especially as opposed to living in a hellhole or being bounced around in foster care.

It is my view that the most important part of the Black family is the Black woman. She is the heart and soul of the Black race, always has been and always will be. Even the horrors and degradation of slavery were unsuccessful in the attempt to destroy her role as anchor of the race. However, areas where slavery failed, crack is succeeding. Often Black women who use crack or cocaine, when they become pregnant rarely stop getting high or seek help. The results are devastating. Black infants whose mothers use during pregnancy are in horrible shape, with low birth rates, multiple handicaps and areas of their brains undeveloped. These are conditions that even slavery could not produce. The Black woman's greatest strength is her spirit. Crack destroys the spirit.

The following poem was originally written for a special Black woman, Paulette, for whom I am forever indebted to. I now offer it to Black women everywhere.

*Black Woman*

The Father above sends us people with love, Someone
    destined to be nice, no matter what the price
When we need them, they are always there and when
    necessary even lead us in prayer Black Woman, this
    is you!!
Your pretty smile turns a gray sky blue
and there are many men who are affected by you but few
    understand you. They see a beautiful sculpture which
    God has created,
So they rush and they push hoping they can be mated …
    with you. Oh, but God has a plan, that only the wise
    understand.
When you extend your hand, it's like water to the land,
    For a chosen few.
Be strong Black woman! I love you.

It is no accident that the crack and cocaine epidemic is most severe in inner city Black neighborhoods where poverty and unemployment are fully entrenched. In the view of many in America, Blacks have always been expendable, second-class citizens. Take a look into the mind of young Black kids in inner city neighborhoods. Well, if they escaped the horrors of mothers using crack they see their playmates gunned down in drive by shootings with the intended targets being rival drug dealers. These kids learn at an early age to live in fear, that the life of a Black person is not considered important and that guns and violence are a way of life in their community. As a result attitudes become hardened and child hoods resemble anything but warm nurturing environments. Drug sales take place right before their eyes, often on school property and in parks and playgrounds. What must we do? Educate, educate, educate! Parents must redirect their social life to revolve around their children, in order for children to see how important they are to the family and as individuals.

Not long ago I was reading an account of the life of Denmark Vescey, a true freedom fighter was he. In the early 1820's he accomplished something that American historians and history books have completely and purposely ignored. He organized an army of 9,000 slaves in South Carolina for rebellion. During this period there were approximately 12,000 slaves and 11,000 whites in South Carolina. His achievement was the most outstanding and daring event by Blacks since arriving in the New World. The plan was told to a slave who as term of the time was, "one who is used to accepting presents of old coats from the master." He informed the local slave owners and Denmark and his key men were taken into custody and hanged. Many people then and today would rather live the role of a slave than be free. Time after time, wherever you look, there goes some Black person eagerly putting down Black people or working against Black people too often shows they will do anything for a dollar or status. These Negroes put a foul smell in the air and always have. One just needs to look at the Koreans, Hispanics, Jews, Arabs, and East Indians. What do they all have common? Here in America each group supports its people economically, politically and socially. The crazy thing about Black people is that many think they can succeed without helping any other Blacks along the way. During the Black movement of the 1960's and 1970's there were a number of Blacks who were very busy actively sabotaging progressive movements and programs in our communities but there kept their actions and identities on the down low for fear of retribution. Now that there is no strong freedom fighting organization in America, there are numerous reactionary fools masquerading as radio talk show hosts, conservatives and Black Republicans openly against affirmative action, actively and publicly anti-black and enjoy maintaining a very high public posture while doing so.

Black consciousness must be resurrected now through the next millennium and directed toward the youth. Amazing as it is, there is very little indication that the 1960's and 1970's has had much impact on the mentality of young Blacks today. Afro-American youth have not sustained an awareness of their culture or social activism. Take a look at Jewish people. They support each other to the maximum. The holocaust is discussed today like it happened yesterday and Jewish leaders never settle for anything less justice regardless of how long it takes to achieve. Afro-Americans must develop the same level of commitment in order to survive. During the civil rights movement, Black ministers were very active in providing physical and financial support. When you look at Black communities across America, the church is an institution you will find in every community regardless of size. Black people definitely believe in going to church. More importantly, what role does the church play in the life of the community today? Unfortunately, many of these churches function is all in-reach and no out-reach.

They collect huge sums of money through donations and provide zero programs or support for the tangible needs of Black youth and the needy.

It is common to see Ministers drive big luxury cars while the churches are often expanding. I remember sitting in a church where the deacons counted the donations and told the pastor the amount. Not satisfied with the total, the pastor told the congregation there would be a special blessing for anyone who would dig deeper into their pockets. Come on!

Unfortunately many people are unable to distinguish when the minister is speaking or when God is speaking through the minister. In the Black community people are constantly asked to attend this or that church. When I am asked that question I say, "Sure I'll attend and what kind of outreach program are you sponsoring?" If I don't get a specific answer, I tell them never mind. Earlier in the book I mentioned the results of a request I made to the pastor in Carbondale, Illinois regarding the need for a breakfast for children program and how all the deacons were against it being housed in their church.

However, the minister was true to his convictions and the ministry and able to stand tall and alone, if necessary. This is a true measure of the commitment a minister has to GOD and community. Churches should be the vanguard in the community just as it was during the time of Christ and operate without fear of confronting the difficult issues of our times. Ministers must come from behind the comfort and walls of their sanctuaries and lead the fight for freedom and justice.

It is time for a change and I maintain that we must start with those among us who are the most well off Black athletes and entertainers must be held to some level of accountability when it comes to the plight of people who suffering among us. It is unacceptable for Black youth to look up to those that have extraordinary talents and wealth and never contribute any money or time to help anyone. I propose the creation of national council of Black athletes, entertainers and corporate giants to set up a structure to provide financial assistance in support of programs for youth, crack babies, the homeless and especially the thousands of black children in foster care around the country to provide a better quality of life and the skills to mainstream and function in society. Such programs would provide clear opportunities for the very fortunate to function as true role models and more often than not, any contributions will end up being tax deductible. We must stop ignoring what people do or don't do simply because they make large sums of money. Have we as a people deteriorated to the level where money determines our code of ethics? Are our concerns and commitments for sale? Just because there are a very few

71

Black people that are making big money does it mean it's okay whatever happens to the masses in our communities? Are police brutality and murder of Black people by white police officers okay when it's happening more frequently now than in the 1960's and 1970's? Out of the ranks of our youth will come those who fight for justice and it will be their task to prevent a watering down of what is acceptable to us and among us as a race of people. Black youth must be recreated in the image of Paul Robeson, Sojourner Truth, W.E.B. Dubois, Harriet Tubman, etc. Have you seen any Black men, who, even remotely resembles a Paul Robeson, or W.E.B. Dubois on the scene today? It is essential that Black youth know the whole truth and nothing but the truth regarding the true nature of this society and how to prepare for tomorrow.

## Follow the Leader and the Leader Is You

Over the years one can look around the world at people who have created their place in history, their place in the sun. Menachem Begin, what did he do? He made bombs and blew up Palestinians but in Israel and world history he is a prime minister, former head of the state of Israel, a world leader. The Irish Republican Army for many years is well known for violence and many, many innocent people died as a result of their actions, but here they are being received around the world, including by the president of the United States, as a legitimate political and governmental organization. However, when Black people, through the Black Panther Party declare, "We want land, bread, housing, education, clothing, justice and peace and furthermore, we will exercise our Second Amendment right to bear arms in self-defense, the Party and people in the movement are considered and treated as thugs, criminals, public enemy No.1, still 3/5 of a man, unworthy of anything but second class citizenship.

All this brings me back to Jimmy, by brother in this life and the next because his spirit resides within me. Upon Jimmy's release from jail we set up for him to go to New York, to a safe house, just off the Columbia University campus. As a matter of fact, he stayed with someone he knew from childhood in Chicago, who was a student at Columbia. For about eight months all went well but his friend began to get paranoid. By this time I went back to Carbondale for the summer to spend some time with a lady friend who had been a rock of support for me. I received a phone call that surprised me but did not shock me. Jimmy had left New York, went to South Florida to a small airfield outside Miami. He approached a pilot of a small plane with a 9mm in hand and demanded that he pilot take him to Cuba. Unfortunately, the pilot refused and Jimmy shot him in the leg, at which point the pilot agreed. I was happy he made it but saddened also. We were all so young and had a lot to learn. However, no one in Black America had ever done what we had done. We were in uncharted waters and we have all paid the price.

Jimmy should not have had to leave the U.S. in the first place. What we had accomplished was so extraordinary but we also needed help. Once we left Carbondale, our base, help was nil. Black Americans as a group, psychologically, physically, and financially, have not and do not up to the present support Black freedom fighters. Our network did not really extend outside of Illinois, although there were those internationally, who supported our struggle in principle. We were faced with the harsh reality of survival in the U.S.A. Many of us had wounds physically and other-wise and had been through a lot to put it mildly, so I make no apologies. The last time I talked to Jimmy, we were both intrigued with going to Angola and fight for the M.P.L.A. the organization that was eventually successful in overthrowing Portuguese colonialism. Therefore I was not surprised of Jimmy being in Cuba. He remained there for about three years and we remained in contact with him by various crew members volunteering for the Venceremos Brigade. An organization in the U.S. that periodically sends mostly progressive young whites, who, volunteer to harvest the sugar cane in Cuba. I believe Jimmy's spirit grew restless and eventually Jimmy and Ida, a sister form California also involved in a plane hijacking from California to Cuba, decided to leave Cuba and go to Jamaica. Castro didn't make anybody who came there, stay in Cuba. You were free to leave but not come back. It's amazing about Fidel and Cuba. Cuba? We're talking about an island that was the play pen of the Cosa Nostra during the 1940's and 1950's. The people were exploited and oppressed with the knowledge and support of the U.S. government. Castro, the leader of the Cuban revolution comes to power and says each

Cuban must be taken care of according to his need, making the gangsters and the U.S. government hostile. One thing for sure is that Castro has always reached out to Black people, in the U.S. and abroad. I remember him coming to New York to speak to the U.N. in the early 1960's. Well, where did he request to stay? He stayed at the Theresa Hotel on the corner of 125th Street and 7th Avenue in the heart of Harlem, where Malcolm, Marcus Garvey, and many Black freedom fighters have always spoke. As a matter of fact when Nelson Mandela was in jail and the ANC was struggling, who was there to support them financially and militarily? Castro and Cuba. When the CIA were helping the South African army in its attempt to keep Angola under Portuguese rule, who was there committing his army, to fight and die in the name of freedom? Castro and Cuba. Black people need to stop reading and listening to the propaganda and become politically sophisticated enough to know who is on which side regarding all matters involving Black people.

At any rate, with Jimmy in Jamaica, things did not go well at all. In an attempt to expropriate money, Jimmy decided to move on a bank. He made a tactical and fatal error. He attempted to disarm the bank guard, who received assistance and Jimmy was shot dead. The FBI licked their lips when they found out that Jimmy had been killed. When the body was flown from Jamaica to the U.S., they mutilated and desecrated his remains. True to form; they must have been crazy or something.

Shortly after Jimmy's death, Ida arrived in New York as a fugitive and true warrior nonetheless. Through support of the people a safe house was obtained for Ida. What amazed me the most about Ida was her strength and determination? There is nothing like being on the run for your life, to keep everything real. I liked her from the moment I met her. She applied for a job as a temp at IBM headquarters in Westchester and when asked if she knew how to operate a specific word processor, she said yes and they hired her. Ida had never even seen a word processor. However, through her relentless tenacity she learned every piece of sophisticated equipment they had. Eventually she bought her own word processor and had a list of clientele including some of the most high powered lawyers and doctors in Westchester County. As a result, she was able to sit at home and make $30 per hour. Yep, my kind of girl. She did this for over nine years often visiting her mother and children in California who were and are her first love. One of her sons who was uninformed in the ways of the world and with behavior problems of his own decided that if he couldn't get what he wanted, when he wanted, that he would turn his mother in. Astonishing, but true. Of course the feds came knocking and off she went to the federal penitentiary in California. What I appreciate the most about Ida is that even in prison for almost 10 years, her spirit and resolve remained high. She was involved in women's rights behind bars and the plight of families and children of women incarcerated. Through the grace of God she was recently released and I truly look forward to greeting her with a giant size hug.

There are many unknown individuals who have sacrificed much for the struggle and we have seen numerous instances of dedicated Black leaders jailed and assassinated due to their unwavering commitment and love for Black people. Malcolm X, Martin Luther King, Fred Hampton, Mark Clark and many, many other lives have been taken, although they remain eternally with us in spirit. Lesser known Black leaders functioning in their communities have been gunned down by police or, is today still in jail serving long and unjust prison terms. It has been historically shown that the very best of our leaders have been isolated and eliminated by the FBI and other branches of law enforcement. We have passed the point where it is viable to look for specific leaders on a national or local level to bear the whole burden of furthering justice and equality for Black people. Each individual must take responsibility for themselves and in order to be an effective and productive human being, regardless of race, an individual must love him or herself. The unfortunate truth is that millions of people do not know how to love themselves. Many Black people have lived with self-hatred which has often been passed down to them from generation to generation. As one develops the ability to truly love self, we become better equipped to communicate and deal with others, which is what all leaders must do. Yes, communication is the key and there are actually three types of communication behaviors; passive, aggressive and assertive. A passive person does not express their needs, feelings or ideas and allows people to infringe on their rights. The aggressive person expresses their feelings and needs at the expense of others and they are often hostile and overpowering. However, the assertive person expresses their feelings and needs without violating the rights of others and that is what it is really all about. We come in contact with each of these kinds of people every day of our lives because all human beings are one of the three. In order to develop leadership qualities it is important to recognize these characteristics in people of all races because one way or another we will have to deal with the consequences of their feelings or actions along with their personal biases and prejudices. Assertiveness often results in achievement, however, when you stand out due to achievement it is not uncommon to run into jealousy, resentment or anger, whether racial or personal. All leaders face some form of this difficulty at one time or another and many people have to deal with it through their lives. When one exhibits leadership qualities it is not uncommon to find someone, somewhere trying to discredit you. When one thinks of the many Black leaders who are no longer here in the flesh, it becomes obvious that leadership must be developed on a grass roots level of "each one teach one." It does not matter whether it is a community project or political action group; it is crucial to be certain in the way one chooses his or her key people.

When a leader of any group chooses his or her people it is always best to start with those individuals who were fully dedicated and supportive during the difficult times. Individuals who made sacrifices out of true commitment should be considered one's key people or base of support.

Strengthen that unit and be content to keep it small and simple. It is essential to take frequent self-inventories to see if we remain worthy of the trust we have been placing in ourselves. We can do this by asking ourselves the following question: Am I acting like a person I can trust? Having trust in and respect for ourselves is the best foundation possible for developing leadership qualities.

In today's racial and political climate it is relevant to make note of what has previously been called the "favorite slave" which was the very opposite type of leader. He derived his powers of leadership from the authority of the master and whose function was to get slaves to accept slavery. They were trusted by the master and could be depended on to personally put down acts of insubordination among the slaves and betray plots for insurrection. Slave plots for revolt were almost always broken up or reported by favorite slaves and frequently the reward of the slaves was money and freedom. The slave that identified himself with the purpose of the white master would derive favors from the master and rise to great esteem among the slaves themselves. Today, that is exactly how Clarence Thomas and others use their slave mentality and actions to be shoved down Black people's throats as a representative of Black people, as if we are supposed to be grateful for being obviously betrayed. It is no surprise that from slavery to the present, the power structure has consistently used Blacks with leadership abilities to counter the activities of Black protest leaders. These Blacks adopt a conservative philosophy and use it for personal gain, rarely involved in a protest in support of Black people. The conservative is always careful not to offend the white power structure and expects to receive material benefits and payment for his support. The conservative Black perfects the submissive approach. The white ruling class assumes the dominant role of establishing the reputation of the Black conservative so-called leader and defends him vigorously against any attacks from Black activist leaders (recall the Clarence Thomas confirmation hearings). It surrounds him with marks of distinction and peddles him as a victorious champion of his people. Clarence Thomas and the many who operate like him are puppets and bootlickers plain and simple. It is crucial for Black people to develop a keen sense of what a true leader is.

Well, we're still not free, regardless of how many millions of dollars a few Black people among us are making. We still don't have the means for guarding and defending ourselves against racist police brutality on the one hand and the drug merchants destroying the very fabric of our communities and our children on the other hand. Yes, it is our children who are being left with this problem because Black men and woman have not raised their voices strong enough to make a difference on these issues. The drug gangs that are presently terrorizing our communities could not have operated during the time that the Black Panther Party was serving the community. The rank and file of the Black Panther Party came of the same class of oppressed young people now operating in the drug trade, unimpeded on our streets today. I believe it will take educated and fearless young people to restore a safe quality of life to our communities. It is up to those of us who care to take a stand and show them the way . . . by any means necessary.

I conclude my text with a poem written for me by one of the most beautiful people I have ever known. It represents the highest honor ever bestowed on me and comes from a sister barely 17 years old, with the knowledge and commitment of a Harriet Tubman. If there was ever someone I would love to see and hug again in this life it is truly Jeri. Rediscovering this poem, which miraculously has survived many moves and relocations around the country over a twenty year period, is very inspiring for me and I use it as a measuring stick to recapture my inner spirit and the Reggie that Jeri knew.

## A Tribute to You

Determined one, sure and convinced Black and extra Proud
Non-organization, but self-organized Comes on like a torpedo
But leaves a track never to be altered, compromised with or destroyed
    Black Man, Comrade, Brother and to some
A lover
My teacher, my example, my drifting, separating lover
Body has been altered, mind semi-confused and emotions played with
    But now body is complete, mind thrives on the spirit of the people
    The will to live and the correct solutions,
And your emotions are back there somewhere But cherished by one
Your theories are proved correct by your practices Young, Black and
    Revolutionary
Dreams are only dreamed while sleep
Reality is the foundation of your awakening, your resting, your
    planning, and our loving
If I could call you anything I'd call you freedom
If I could paint you a certain color I'd paint you the color of a silver
    bullet If I could give anything it wouldn't be myself as I now stand
It would be my ideas in practice And when I no longer see or feel you
I will take on my role of covering your tracks
Your will to strike down Oppression will forever prevail over all those
    You've ever spoken to, worked with or make love to
And at the highest point of emotions your mind carried you
    righteously to deal With after affects, realities and circumstance
Yes, and at times of frustration with you, my mind was pushed into a
    corner But that corner showed me some rays of light
Some rays of light which made me admire you even more To speak of
    time is to utter your name
For you have never wasted time

*A Tribute to You*

You have taught me the meaning of struggling and how to deal with
    it From your knowledge I have gained my knowledge, priorities,
    discipline
and to love all who practice their theories
I have gained the knowledge of getting rid of certain ideals which
    only served to hinder our cause You have been and will be more
    important than any teacher or preacher
has ever been to me For you are a Black Man
Your body belongs to, not me or her
or even him, but to the masses of people So in tribute to you and your
    accomplishments
I have composed this incomplete work from my soul Incomplete
    because of your ever advancing position

## *Rap Up*

A little something extra for the youth because they are the future, our
future

═══════════════════════════════════════════

## *Changing Times*

As we head into this new millennium we must stay connected to our
    roots
That's why . . . I drop jewels like the morning dew
Wake up! Let your mind rise like the sun for a sneak preview Aahh,
    mental effervescence
Bringing you the lessons from the past, the now and the future too I
    got mad prophesies to reveal to you
We left 1999
And there are very few warriors still battling on the front lines Gone
    are the days when kids can play
In front of their house or on the way to school Yeah even if they make
They don't get taught cause the teachers are faking it Messing with our
    kids minds
Trying to discourage them and leaving them behind Hell yeah, there's
    rage in our community
The only thing short is real unity But hold on, the time has come
To confront the problem and add up the sum We didn't get the 40 aces
    and 2 mules
I'll get to that in a minute but here are some new rules
First one starts right in the home
Brothers making babies and leaving them alone Rule #1 in this has got
    to stop
Anyone doing that might as well be . . . kaplow! Woow! I know that's a
    harsh solution
But brothers like that are creating pollution In the hearts and spirits of
    our young minds
And both parents in the home is now hard to find Who's gonna take
    the weight?
Who's gonna make it plain?
And drop jewels on the brothers and sisters Get em hip to the game
    the way it's being played Rule #2 is to educate

Most of our people don't know how to relate And a people without a
culture are easily persuaded Ignorant, confused and often hated
But the worst hate starts from within
If you don't like yourself there's nothing you can win Now about those
acres and mules
You get nothing in this world unless you enforce the rules
"Power concedes nothing without demand" was said by Frederick
Douglas Now there's not one Mr. Douglas among us
But hold on each one teach one
Raise up the people, create some new sons
And daughters too
God knows we wouldn't be anywhere without you So sisters keep
shining and walking the walk
Any man out there can talk the talk Be in control of your destiny
Or else you'll be saying, "damn, he got the best of me Who's gonna
take the weight
Who's gonna make it plain
Drop jewels on the brothers and sisters
Get them hop to the game the way it's being played Yo, it's time for a
new way of thinking
A new way to look and a new way of speaking Check it, the Klan is still
lynching blacks Saying "them scared niggers won't react"
Stop forgiving those who don't deserve forgiveness If you do they're
gonna give you the business Disrespect and walk all over you
We've got to throw out the old and bring in the new Well it's new for
those just beginning to hear it Take a stand for our lives, no way
we're gonna fear it All real warriors meet me on the front!
We need a few good men fit to lead a real hunt Fakes and phonies close
the doors
Here comes the fury, you better hit the floor!
Oh yeah, clear sounds of changing times New direction and new
meaning to the rhyme
The first became last and now the last again is first This new world
order is sure good for the thirst The original people back again on
top
Don't even imagine that we're gonna stop It was all predestined for this
to happen

*Changing Times*

Soaring like an eagle hear the sound of gun-clapping To make a
    comeback you do it over time
But we were only extinct in the depths of our minds
You know, there are brothers and sisters in jail and on the run For over
    30 years for crimes they haven't done
Departed warriors, Fred Hampton, Jonathan Jackson, to you they're a
    mystery That's because we let others write our history
Never let someone pick your heroes for you It only makes it easy for
    them to destroy you Special shout out to Assata Shakur
Who already has a place in Black Folklore

## *History of the Heights*

During the American Revolution there were big time fights And old
president George won his bragging rights

In the North part of Manhattan, George burned the candlelight That's
why they call it Washington Heights

Here was his headquarters, he made plans for battle And now in
history sits tall in the saddle

But I'm here to tell you what has really gone down Since way back
when old George was around

Yo, when I was coming up the Heights was real cool In the streets we
had games to play after school Tops, lodies, run catch and kiss

Chase the girl of your dreams and then fulfill a wish Then in the late
60's came the French Connection Heroin spreading like it was an
infection

Matter of fact, Panthers called the plague Junkies shooting it in their
arm, neck and legs That's when the Heights really began to change
And since then it's never been the same

In the 70's and 80's things kept going down Then, Oh shit, crack came
around

Crack's from pedico and it's probably here to stay But I'm here to tell
you who's calling the big plays The commanders, the generals are
from Dominicana

And the Heights is where you'll see them manana Yo, the truth is with
them I'm real cool

The history of their lives would fill up this school They come from a
land of real poverty

And will do what it takes for them to be free In the Heights they got
pedico all locked down

And there's more in the Heights than any city around The whole
country, yes the USA

And if it's about pedico they're the ones you've got to pay But 156th
Street is still my block

I visit old friends regardless of the clock But the truth is, there's only a
few around

Some have moved but most are in the ground And if old George could
come back he'd really flip

The candle they used to burn would be used to take a hit Yeah, I won't
lie I got caught up in the drama

Pedico was to me what corn is to the farmer Upstairs, third floor,
gonna get the package Heart beating fast, pocket full of cabbage
Shotgun, Uzi, in the back room

Want to hurry up before something goes boom!

Could be coming from the back or tactical squad at the door Will do
you no good just to hit the floor

Cause in the middle of a big drug play

You could go to jail or meet your maker that day So far so good
everything's quiet

But I would feel better if this was at the Hyatt "Papi, this for you, ok?"

"Yeah, that looks real cool, gracias" Now let me hurry and get to the
car

I'm parked around the corner, it ain't that far

Couple of freaks in the hallway want me to take em, uh, uh All I'm
hoping is I won't be forsaken

Made it to the car and I'm on the highway Feeling real lucky like I was
OJ

This is the Heights 24/7

And cops feeling like they died and went to heaven When they roll up
on dealers and shake them down They're guaranteed to see plenty
g's hit the ground It's the Heights y'all, belee that

## *The Letter*

Damn, here I go again
It's my 2nd bid in just three years
Things I thought I knew now don't seem so clear You really lose focus
  when you're in jail
I'm starting to feel inhuman but at least I got mail I read this letter
  from my homeboy Chad
I thought I'd feel better, it only made me mad Peace bro,
Things on the home front ain't real good Only thing worse is
  conditions in the hood My little sister split and my mom's on crack
  Was gone three days, said she'd be right back When she showed up
  she brings a nigga home I come real close to putting a nine in his
  dome I could kill my mom too but I love her so
It tears me up to see her stoop so low
Well the money's coming quick and once in a while there's a bust Got
  people around me but nobody I really trust
I watch them honeys too cause they be scheming The set you up quick
  if you're daydreaming Just a few years ago we were both young
No matter what we did it was always a bunch of fun Now I'm 22 and
  got the world on my shoulders
You'd think I'd be happy slinging rocks big as boulders I just put a
  grand in the canteen for you
And I'll give you credit your girl Renee still adores you But the truth is
  I don't think she'll wait
Five long years just to meet you at the gate Nothing personal against
  you, that's just the way it is Most girls get busy while there man's
  doing bids Man, why didn't you just stay in school
You was the smartest in the class, had all the tools But you started
  slinging rocks while on full scholarship Trying to be the answer to
  your family's hardships Now that Pre-med shit is just a thing of the
  past

You got impatient and wanted quick cash But yo, I had to use the
streets just to survive

Got tired of being hungry, made moves to stay alive You'd think with
all this money I'd feel real good

I guess that's on me because I really should Everyone in my family
always been hard Remember, both my brothers died living large
The streets took their lives, is my mom next Or is it me that's
getting ready to be put to rest

In a way I don't care cause life stopped being fun When I realized I
never had a dad call me son

I got to roll up a fat one to deal with all these feelings

But even that and this Hennessy don't bring no healing You know you
my man, we could always talk

You had knowledge for everyone but on you. Yu came up short I was
really depending on you to stay legit

So when the time came I could just quit These streets put my money
on something safe But instead my money just builds up in my safe
On the real,

All the money out there ain't meant to be taken

The biggest deals are often the ones where you're mistaken When it
comes to street money it's all systematic

There's only two parts, the dealer and the addict Remember the old-
timer Big Mike from way back He made moves all them years and
never got cracked Mike always said "I'll take the fortune not the
fame" No flashing, no jewelry, he always looked the same

Most young boys making money want you to know they got it Then it's
not long before they're real hot

Not cause "one time" knows what's brewing Jealousy and envy become
their undoing

I'm canceling on people, moving on the down low Got enough stashed
to make a little and go slow I don't if I'll be around when you get
out

Any given day I could go down for the count

So, remember we're all responsible for the choices that we make If it
don't go right, then these are the breaks

Peace, Chad

## Charleston Experience

How does a Black kid get promoted to 8th grade? And he can't even
   read the word say
He's had Black teachers all throughout school With no conscience
   about making a child a fool Damn, I don't know how they sleep at
   night!
Seeing this kid suffer was a pitiful sight
And if you talk to the parents, they say everything's fine Cause they're
   happy collecting his SSI
Told me to be cool; they don't want to cause no problem But I'm about
   pushing up and showing how to solve 'em This kid lives below the
   Mason Dixon line
And he'd damn sue be reading if he were mine
The song says "nothing can be finer than to be in Carolina" But the
   Blacks taking more shit than an ocean liner
OK. I'll be cool, on that I'll close
This shit's got me heated, I need a water hose

## Looking Back

We stand alone—The Carbondale 6.

We go down in history as the only group of people, only cell, only crew, only cadre, only organization, yes the only ones that waged armed,. Struggle against police; as a matter of fact against multiple police jurisdictions simultaneously without breaking the law. We were able to do something that perhaps nobody thought was possible. My dad always says "it aint bragging when you can back it up."

*Pinnacle*—the point of greatest success or achievement.

*Peak*—suggests the highest of other high points. Yeah, I like the way both those words sound.

When anyone who claims to work for the betterment of Black America come in contact with me or any member of the Carbondale 6, they should salute because we are generals in the struggle. As founder of the Cadre, I put together a crew that fought the heaviest armed battle of the civil rights era while simultaneously creating programs that gave power to the people and firmly developed strong support in the white community especially among mother country radicals.

I have a responsibility to let the world know, let America know, let Black America know that Carbondale, Illinois is the site of Black America's "Battle of the Little Big Horn." Police jurisdictions from all over Southern Illinois took part in the "Battle of Carbondale" and we battled them to a draw and that's a solid win for us, for the struggle and for generations to come. The way the Black community rallied to support the Carbondale 6 was poetry in motion; marching out of their homes demanding the police initiate an immediate ceasefire and select members of the community went in the house to arrange the surrender.

Yeah, yeah, a political education experience, no props, live bullets only. It's really fascinating to look back and see "Power to the People" in action.

As I do an objective self-evaluation I recognize many significant achievements and various paradoxical hard to ignore issues and flaws. For one, I have from childhood always been concerned about acceptance and worrying about what others thought of me, yes my image. And it is that worrying about image one time too many that brought me to the brink of death. In reality I shouldn't have been concerned one way or another when asked to do that fateful mission. Saying, "Hell no, I am not getting down with that" should have been easy as hell considering that I had no prior contact or experience with those materials.

What is permanently etched into my memory is the fact that the clown who gave me the explosives visited me recovering at my mom and dad's home in New York. He came into the bedroom with another individual then went back to the living room and never spoke to me in private and I know if it had been me I would have been in a crazy hurry to say, "yo man what the fuck happened;" I also would have asked if anyone knew that I provided those materials to you. Looks like a hit to me, but why? I conclude jealousy. When I look at other people it's like you can have all of this and all of that and so what? It means zero to me because I am unconcerned about what other people have or do for a living. However it is unfortunate in this world that there are many people who have an obsession to be "top dog" and some go to the extreme when it is perceived that a certain individual is in the way. Keen insight is needed when dealing with obsessive, deceptive people. One must stick to the rules and Rule N0.1 is when someone comes to you and says, do this operation and you realize you are being asked to do something, they wouldn't do themselves, your personal alarm system should go off, because that is a big red flag right there. In 45 years this snake has never reached out to me or enquired about my health and wellbeing, not even once. Using simple math, that adds up to a "hit" right there.

You know I look back at the mission given me by the Venerable Fred Hampton to bring a Panther presence to the Southern Region of the state which we did and some. "The Battle of Carbondale" is the result of young Afro-American men, teenagers when we started who gave their all, to fight for freedom from oppression and we did it because of our love for the people and if we hadn't, then who would?

The documentary 778 Bullets is a welcome validation of some of our many accomplishments and I identify and accept a responsibility to help put the legacy of the Carbondale 6 in its proper and well deserved place in history. We were the People's Army. When the White Hat's vigilantes terrorized the Black Housing Project Pyramid Court in Cairo, Illinois the call went out for help and before you can blink, we were there doing armed security patrols.

I will never accept Afro-Americans being relegated to an unclear and false place in history. Furthermore, when it comes to Afro-American Freedom Fighters it seems that information is often blurry and incomplete. There has always been a concerted effort to ignore and bury the achievements of Black American Freedom fighters. However, you can probably go in any school in America and ask the student if they have ever heard of Geronimo and most can tell you he is an Indian Warrior held in great reverence by Native Americans not surprisingly blacks were slow to acknowledge and appreciate Malcolm's greatness until long after his death. However, I can tell you this; the legacy of the Carbondale 6 is going to be right up there at the top where it belongs as the best of the best. From now to eternity I envision and prophesize that there will never be another case in American history of anyone having a shootout with police, where officers are wounded, police cars severely damaged, individuals go to trial, found not guilty of all changes and given back every last one of their weapons; and for just those reasons, right there, WE STAND ALONE.

Google 778 Bullets—yeah and Google it over and over. You know it's a funny thing about Afro-American Freedom Fighters. When prominent Blacks acknowledge the Black Panther Party, it stirs up backlash and economic boycott of said Blacks in order to intimidate and isolate any Black showing that support and respect for the Black Panther Party. One thing Black people are always going to desperately need is knowledge of self.

No Black people should ever allow anyone to scare them away from showing Homage for the Freedom Fighters. It's my goal and hope that all black youth know about the Carbondale 6. Google 778 Bullets.

I bow my head in remembrance of Brother Rab who passed recently. Rab's courageous effort going back in the house to pull me out is the reason I am alive today. Brother you are sorely missed and never forgotten. Brother Jimmy, although you left us long ago, that you are the best of the best I will always know. And I always knew you were a winner from the get go.

Well, it was 45 years ago that a nurse took a courageous stand in deciding to accompany me in my plane ride to Freedom. I call it that because I could not survive the trip without her care. Her dedication, courage and compassion in my mind is second to none. Dear Ms. Goodman I love you always and forever. I send you a spiritual hug and I will never ever let go. Peace and love to you always.

That brings me to my final entry. I know that we all have regrets and I have many but what often haunts me is how much I miss my Mom and Dad. I feel anger and shame that I often didn't recognize my Dad's greatness and wisdom. For him to be able to come to Carbondale and connect with someone who assisted in providing the plane that flew me to Freedom is more than extraordinary. Yes, my special, special Dad, I live my life in remembrance of you and Mom.

To the very special gentleman who connected with my father and delivered a plane with pilot and co-pilot, Man you are the best!

And to the town and people of Carbondale, I love you always and forever.

CARBONDALE 6

PRE-EMINENT AFRO AMERICAN FREEDOM

FIGHTERS OF THE 20TH CENTURY